An Orange Tree Theatre and Up in
in association with Reading Rep

German S
BY ROBERT HOLM.

C000192556

German Skerries was first presented at the Bush Theatre, London,
on 25 January 1977.

This production was first presented at the Orange Tree Theatre,
Richmond on the 3 March 2016, with the following cast:

Jack Williams **GEORGE EVANS**
Martin Jones **HOWARD WARD**
Michael Haddaway **HENRY EVERETT**
Carol Williams **KATIE MOORE**

Director **ALICE HAMILTON**
Designer **JAMES PERKINS**
Lighting Designer **SIMON GETHIN THOMAS**
Sound Designer & Composer **GEORGE DENNIS**
Dialect Coach **MARK LANGLEY**
Casting Consultant **CHARLOTTE SUTTON**

Production Manager **NICK MAY**
Costume Supervisor **VICTORIA SMART**
Stage Manager & Company Stage Manager on Tour **TARA CLAXTON**
Deputy Stage Manager **CHARLIE YOUNG**

Thanks to Bob and Eric and the London Wetland Centre

UP IN ARMS

Artistic Directors | **Alice Hamilton** and **Barney Norris**
Producer | **Chloe Courtney**
Resident Stage Manager | **Charlie Young**

Honest, human, affecting, revealing: we make plays about people and the places they're from.

Up in Arms makes theatre to reveal what is extraordinary about people's ordinary lives. In the last two years the company's work has featured in theatre of the year lists from *The Times*, the *Guardian*, the *Evening Standard*, *The Arts Desk* and *The Stage*, and garnered numerous awards. Whether touring to the UK's leading theatres, its areas of lowest cultural engagement or communities particularly affected by issues in their work, the company's project is always the same: to engage people emotionally with the conditions of their lives and the lives being lived around them.

Our audiences make us who we are.

We'd particularly like to acknowledge the contribution of our Supporters:

Very Special Thanks to Frank and Elizabeth Brenan, Alison Lowdon, Sarah, Pete and Ruth Shepherd, Peter and Jane Hamilton.

Special Thanks to Offline Magazine, Rachel Bebb, Susanna Bishop, Farhana Bhula, Shabana Bhula, Richard Broyd, John Cox, Veronica Dewan, Bekah Diamond, Hasan Dixon, Esther Ruth Elliott, John Foster, Victoria Gee, Hannah Groombridge, Anna Hamilton and Angus Meryon, Juliette Kelly-Fleming, Suzy McClintock, Alice Malin, Linda Morse, Frank Newhofer, Janet Rieder, Stephanie Ressort, Celia Swan.

Thanks to the Workers Educational Association, Lindsay Balkwell and Ivan Richardson, Sarah Blake, Cassie Bradley, Sophia Chetin-Leuner, Natalie Denton, Milly Ellis, Aidan Grounds, Barbara Houseman, Luke Holbrook, Louisa Hollway, Katharine Ingle, Max Lindsay, Alex Orchard-Lisle, George Nichols, Naomi Petersen, Kandy Rohmann, Josie Underwood, George Warren.

You can find out more about becoming a Supporter at **upinarms.org.uk**

KEEP IN TOUCH – JOIN OUR MAILING LIST
Online **upinarms.org.uk**
Twitter **@upinarmstheatre**
Facebook **Up In Arms**
Instagram **upinarmstheattre**

Supported using public funding by
ARTS COUNCIL ENGLAND
LOTTERY FUNDED

Orange Tree Theatre

The Orange Tree Theatre aims to stir, delight, challenge, move and amaze with a bold and continually evolving mix of new and re-discovered plays in our unique in-the-round space. We want to change lives by telling remarkable stories from a wide variety of times and places, filtered through the singular imagination of our writers and the remarkable close-up presence of our actors.

A theatre of this scale, with the audience wrapped around the players, invites acting to be the centre of the experience. This is theatre as a figurative art: the human being literally at its centre. We want to experience voices and stories from our past and our present alongside visions of the future. Life as it's lived: unplugged and unmiked. Close-up magic. Truths the hand can touch.

Over its 44-year history the Orange Tree has had a very strong track record in discovering writers and promoting their early work, as well rediscovering artists from the past whose work had either been disregarded or forgotten. Over the past eighteen months the work of Terence Rattigan, Doris Lessing, Mustapha Matura, Bernard Shaw, Sharman Macdonald and DH Lawrence has played alongside new work by Alistair McDowall, Alice Birch, Deborah Bruce and Adam Barnard.

COMING SOON

7 – 30 APRIL

The Brink
A NEW PLAY BY BRAD BIRCH

12 MAY – 25 JUNE

The Philanderer
BY BERNARD SHAW

30 JUNE – 30 JULY

French Without Tears
BY TERENCE RATTIGAN

orangetreetheatre.co.uk
020 8940 3633

Artistic Director **Paul Miller**   Executive Director **Sarah Nicholson**

The Orange Tree is a registered charity (no. 266128) and is generously supported by the London Borough of Richmond upon Thames.

German Skerries
2016 Tour Dates

3 March - 2 April
Orange Tree Theatre, Richmond
orangetreetheatre.co.uk | 020 8940 3633

6 - 9 April
Reading Rep
Readingrep.com | 01189 554 757

13 - 16 April
Stephen Joseph Theatre, Scarborough
Sjt.uk.com | 01723 370 541

20 - 21 April
Dukes Theatre, Lancaster
Dukes-lancaster.org | 01524 598 500

22 - 23 April
Hull Truck Theatre
Hulltruck.co.uk | 01482 323638

Lines Of Desire

Robert Holman's *German Skerries* is a portrait of being alive as being unmoored. We are introduced to four people buffeted by the winds of the world: bird watchers observing ships coming in and pipes being laid as the roar of the future drowns their coastline. From our vantage point in 2016, the way that weather lashes them is all the more poignant. Holman didn't know it, but his play chronicles the last breaths Redcar took before Thatcher; we didn't plan it, but we're staging it in the first few months after the steel plant was shut down, the blast furnace turned off. Trapped in the amber of the script, something in the way the characters address the world seems to see it all coming, the way things will be out of their hands:

> JACK. We're being told there's a depression, I don't see much of it about. I try to understand what I can.

As Michael, the character whose life is most dramatically overturned by the big world in this story, has cause to reflect, most of life seems to go on without us all, far beyond our understanding or control: 'You're supposed to know the answer, aren't you. When everything is put in its place. Well, at the end of the day I don't know any more than I did before.' Everyone in the play seems keenly aware of how much bigger the world is than their experience of it. You hear it in Martin's observation of the cormorant in flight: 'there's no man on earth could do that.' The marvellousness of what's around Martin and the cloudiness besetting Michael's understanding are the same thing, an apprehension of the vastness of their surroundings.

From this insight, Holman weaves a study of the limits of lives, the way we're bounded by circumstance into little more than a stone's throw of experience. His characters dream:

> JACK. When I was a kid, I 'ad this dream. T'put all me stuff in a JCB an' drive off. Roamin' thee ole world. All I 'ad t'do was put a clean shirt in the scoop. Sounds daft dun it?

But dreaming is all they ever plan to do about it.

> JACK. You know what I'm gonna tell my kiddies? About ambition? You see, it doesn't matter if you do anythin' about yer ambitions, so long as you've 'ad 'em. Then you've always got something to think about.

Attempting to exceed one's own little lot seems, on this spit of
land and far from everything, like an act of breathless audacity. No
one understands this with more urgency than Carol, cast by her
environment as the supporter of her husband Jack. She tries to
bring the good in him into the light, but can't really be sure it's the
right thing she's doing:

> CAROL. I sometimes feel I'm pushing you into things.
> JACK. Lamp posts?
> CAROL. You know what I mean.

The play shows two young people encountering the outer limits of
their dreaming for the first time, and wondering how they might be
able to extend them; another man who has found ways to keep his
dream life alive; and a man who hasn't, who is lost in the quotidian,
dragged deep under into worry and regret.

What's extraordinary about *German Skerries* is that this is just the
beginning of the play's achievement. By recording these dreamers,
Holman is also performing an act of rescue, detailing ways of life
that might disappear completely if he didn't write them down, desire
lines which appear on no other map of the world. Even within the
confines of the play, the story that led to the rocks at the mouth
of the Tees being called the German skerries is already vanishing,
stored 'in an archive somewhere', known by very few. And I think
he performs an act of politicised worship as well: in celebrating the
small rituals and patterns of one culture, giving love to one world, he
offers the idea that all lives and cultures are precious and important,
to be celebrated in all the uniqueness of their different rhythms.
Martin asks, 'I often wonder why we have to be concerned with the
way we all live – I don't know why we don't just get on with it.' The
play around him knows the answer. It is in concerning ourselves with
the lives of others that we might see a way to living more completely.
Holman's play shows us people on the edge of life – on the brink
and diving in, but also at the margin. For the duration of an evening
at the theatre, he puts them at the centre of the world. And perhaps
he asks us to consider that the double meaning I'm proposing for
their marginality, the simultaneous sense of something precipitous
and knife-edged and something far-flung, might be central to all our
experiences of life: that we're all adrift in the same boat.

Barney Norris, 2016

Company Biographies

Tara Claxton | Stage Manager
At the Orange Tree: *The Distance* (and Sheffield Theatres).
Other theatre includes: *Five Finger Exercise* (The Print Room); *How To Be A Hero* (Albany/ Birmingham Rep); *Beautiful Thing* (UK tour for QNQ Ltd/Leicester Curve/ Nottingham Playhouse); *Ali Baba* (Chipping Norton Theatre); *Chris Dugdale: 2Faced Deception* (Leicester Square Theatre/ Riverside Studios); *Collision* (Hackney Empire); *The Lady in the Van, The Importance of Being Earnest, Bogus Woman, Spring Awakening, History Boys, A Doll's House, The Railway Children, Roma and the Flannelettes, The Comedy of Errors, An Inspector Calls, Peter Pan* (Theatre By The Lake, Keswick).

George Dennis | Sound Designer & Composer
With Up In Arms: *Eventide* (Arcola and tour); *Visitors* (Bush Theatre and tour).

Theatre includes: *The Homecoming* (Jamie Lloyd Company/Trafalgar Studios); *Fireworks, Liberian Girl, Primetime (Royal Court); Brave New World, Regeneration* (Royal and Derngate/Touring Consortium); *Forget Me Not* (Bush Theatre); *Image of an Unknown Young Woman, Eclipsed, The Edge of our Bodies* (Gate Theatre); *Harrogate* (HighTide Festival); *Chicken* (Eastern Angles/Unity Theatre); *Beautiful Thing* (Arts Theatre/UK Tour); *A Breakfast of Eels, The Last Yankee* (Print Room); *peddling* (Arcola Theatre/59E59, New York/HighTide Festival); *Mametz* (National Theatre of Wales); *Minotaur* (Polka Theatre/Clwyd Theatr Cymru); *Spring Awakening* (Headlong); *The Island* (Young Vic); *Love Your Soldiers* (Sheffield Crucible Studio); *Thark* (Park Theatre); *Moth* (Bush Theatre/HighTide Festival); *Hello/ Goodbye* (Hampstead Theatre); *Liar Liar* (Unicorn Theatre); *Good Grief* (Theatre Royal Bath/UK Tour); *The Seven Year Itch* (Salisbury Playhouse); *When Did You Last See My Mother?* (Trafalgar Studios 2); *Debris, The Seagull, The Only True History of Lizzie Finn* (Southwark Playhouse); *A Life, Foxfinder* (Finborough Theatre).

George Evans | Jack
Theatre includes: *The Shawshank Redemption* (Bill Kenwright Ltd., UK tour); *American Buffalo* (Wyndham's Theatre); *Three Winters* (National Theatre); *Missing* (Belgrade/Old Vic Tunnels); *The Importance Of Being Earnest* (English Theatre of Hamburg); *The Sea Plays* (Old Vic Tunnels).

TV includes: *Hollyoaks.*

Film includes: *Richard II.*

Henry Everett | Michael
At the Orange Tree: *The Suitcase Kid.*
Theatre includes: *Richard II* (Globe Theatre); *Man and Superman* (National

Theatre); *A Midsummer Night's Dream* (Michael Grandage Company); *The Nutcracker* (Theatre Royal Bath); *Sold* (Theatre503); *All Creatures Great and Small* (Gala Theatre, Durham); *My Brother the Robot* (Tall Stories); *Autobahn* (King's Head); *Fool for Love, Reigen* (GBS Theatre, RADA); *The Cherry Orchard* (Dog Orange); *The Taming of the Shrew, The Importance of Being Earnest, The Comedy of Errors, The Merry Wives of Windsor, Macbeth* (Oxford Shakespeare Company); *A Christmas Carol* (Shaw Theatre); *Private Lives, Dead of Night* (Sheringham Little Theatre); *Sleeping Beauty* (The Roses, Tewkesbury); *Lovers From Hell* (Oval House Theatre); *The Merry Wives of Windsor* (Changeling Theatre Company); *I-Confess* (Tangled Feet).

TV includes: *Filth: the Mary Whitehouse Story, Emmerdale, The Bill, Switch, Routes.*

Film includes: *WMD, Milk Man.*

Alice Hamilton | Director
Alice is the co-artistic director of Up in Arms. Direction for the company includes *Eventide* (Arcola and tour), *Visitors* (Bush, Arcola and tour), *Fear of Music* (Up in Arms/Out of Joint tour) and *At First Sight* (Latitude Festival and tour). Other theatre includes *Orson's Shadow* (Southwark Playhouse). She worked as Staff Director on *Man and Superman* at the National Theatre, and has assisted on shows at Northampton Royal and Derngate, Liverpool Playhouse, Hampstead Theatre and Trafalgar Studios.

Robert Holman | Writer
Robert Holman's is a renowned and celebrated playwright in British Theatre. His plays include: *Mud* (Royal Court, 1974); *Rooting* (Traverse, 1979); *Other Worlds* (Royal Court, 1980); *Today* (RSC, 1984); *The Overgrown Path* (Royal Court, 1985); *Making Noise Quietly* (Bush, 1987, and revived at the Donmar, 2012); *Across Oka* (RSC, 1988); *Rafts and Dreams* (Royal Court, 1990); *Bad Weather* (RSC, 1998); *Holes in the Skin* (Chichester Festival Theatre, 2003); *Jonah And Otto* (Royal Exchange Theatre, 2008, and revived at the Park Theatre, 2014); and *A Thousand Stars Explode in the Sky* (co-written with David Eldridge and Simon Stephens, Lyric Hammersmith, 2010). Most recently his play *A Breakfast of Eels* premiered at the Print Room (2015). Robert has been Resident Dramatist at the National Theatre and RSC. He has also written for television and radio.

Katie Moore | Carol
Theatre includes: *The Funfair* (Home, Manchester); *Billy Liar* (Manchester Royal Exchange); *The Little Mermaid* (Bristol Old Vic); *England Street* (Oxford Playhouse); *Salad Days* (Riverside Studios); *Swallows And Amazons* (Vaudeville Theatre and UK tour); *The Glass Menagerie* (New Vic Theatre).

TV includes *Call The Midwife, The Paradise, Doc Martin, Misfits, Merlin, Doctors.*

Film includes *Icarus Time And The Edge Of Destiny.*

James Perkins | Designer

With Up in Arms: *Eventide* (Arcola and tour).

Other theatre includes: *The Last Five Years* (New Wolsey Theatre); *The Gathered Leaves, Out Of The Cage* (Park Theatre); *Little Shop Of Horrors* (Royal Exchange, Manchester); *Breeders* (St James Theatre); *Shiver, Lost In Yonkers* (Watford Palace Theatre); *Ciphers* (Bush Theatre/Out Of Joint); *1001 Nights* (Unicorn Theatre/Transport Theatre); *Liar Liar* (Unicorn Theatre); *The Girl In The Yellow Dress* (Salisbury Playhouse); *Microcosm* (Soho Theatre); *Dances of Death* (Gate Theatre); *The Fantasist's Waltz* (York Theatre Royal); *Stockwell* (Tricycle Theatre); *Carthage, Foxfinder, Events While Guarding The Bofors Gun, Trying* (Finborough Theatre); *The Only True History Of Lizzie Finn, Floyd Collins* (Southwark Playhouse); *The Marriage Of Figaro* (Wilton's Music Hall); *The Life Of Stuff, Desolate Heaven, Threads, Many Moons* (Theatre503); *The Hotel Plays* (Grange Hotel); *St John's Night, Saraband* (Jermyn Street Theatre); *The Pirates of Penzance, HMS Pinafore* (Buxton Opera House); *Matters Of Life And Death* (Contemporary Dance UK Tour); *Iolanthe, The Way Through The Woods* (Pleasance Theatre, London); *The Faerie Queen* (Lilian Baylis, Sadler's Wells); *The Wonder* (BAC). James created Story Whores. He is an associate of Forward Theatre Project and one third of paper/scissors/stone.

Victoria Smart | Costume Supervisor

Victoria trained in Design for Performance at Wimbledon College of Art. Previous costume work and supervising includes: *P'yongyang* (Finborough Theatre) *Oliver!* (Curve, Leicester) and *The Life of Stuff* (Theatre503). Design credits include *Enduring Song* (Southwark Playhouse); *The Last March* (Bikeshed/ Southwark Playhouse); *Maria 1968* (Edinburgh Fringe); and *Billy Chickens is a Psychopath Superstar* (Theatre 503 at Latitude). She also works as a prop and modelmaker and collaborates on artist led projects.

Charlotte Sutton | Casting Consultant

Theatre includes: *Waiting for Godot* (Sheffield Theatres); *Goodnight Mister Tom* (Duke of York's & tour - for ATG); *Mack and Mabel* (Chichester Festival Theatre & tour); *wonder.land* (Manchester International Festival & National Theatre); *Little Shop of Horrors* (Salisbury Playhouse); Queen Coal (Sheffield Theatres); *Albion* (Bush Theatre); *The Light Princess, Emil and the Detectives, The Elephantom* (National Theatre); *Twelfth Night Re-Imagined* (Regent's Park Open Air Theatre); *One Man, Two Guvnors* (Theatre Royal Haymarket recasts); *The Rise and Shine of Comrade Fiasco, I'd Rather Goya Robbed Me of My Sleep Than Some Other A*sehole, Gruesome Playground Injuries* (Gate); *Our Big Land* (New Wolsey, Ipswich, and tour); *Forever House* (Drum Theatre, Plymouth); *Cabaret* (Savoy & National Tour); *Desire Under the Elms* (Lyric Hammersmith); *Not Another Musical* (Latitude Festival); *Run! A Sports Day Musical* (Polka Theatre); *Shivered* (Southwark Playhouse); *The Tour Guide* (Edinburgh Festival); *Bunny* (Underbelly, Edinburgh/Soho Theatre/59E59, NY) and *First Lady Suite* (Union Theatre).

Simon Gethin Thomas | Lighting Designer
With Up In Arms: *Eventide* (Arcola and tour); *Visitors* (Bush Theatre, Arcola and tour), *Fear Of Music* (tour with Out Of Joint).

Other theatre includes: *Rent* (Birmingham School of Acting); *Eye Of A Needle* (Gutshot Productions/Southwark Playhouse); *Pincher Martin* (Britten Theatre, RCM); *Othello: Deconstructed* (Oxford School of Drama).

Howard Ward | Martin
Theatre includes *Monsieur Popular* (Theatre Royal Bath); *Pride And Prejudice* (Sheffield Crucible); *NT 50, London Road, The Good Hope, The Mysteries, Johnny On The Spot* (National Theatre); *The Curious Incident of the Dog In The Night Time* (National Theatre and Apollo Theatre); *War Horse* (National Theatre/New London Theatre); *Jack And The Beanstalk* (Lyric Hammersmith); *A Walk On Part* (Soho Theatre/Live Theatre); *The Changeling* (Young Vic); *The Golden Dragon* (ATC); *Wanderlust, Incomplete And Random Acts Of Kindness, Night Owls, A Day In Dull Armour* (Royal Court); *Henry V, Much Ado About Nothing* (RSC); *The English Game* (Headlong); *A Couple Of Poor, Polish Speaking Romanians* (Soho Theatre); *Heartbreak House, Neville's Island* (Watford Palace Theatre); *How Long Is Never?, Fabulation* (Tricycle); *Under The Black Flag* (Shakespeare's Globe); *The Prayer Room* (Birmingham Rep); *Six Degrees Of Separation* (Manchester Royal Exchange); *King Arthur* (Theatre Du Chatelet).

TV includes *Downton Abbey, Lady Chatterley's Lover, Midsomer Murders, Parade's End, Toast, Doctors, Casualty, The Bill, Ghost Squad, Panorama - Blair On Trial, Heartbeat, The Government Inspector, Crisis Command, Family Affairs, Absolute Power, Amnesia, M.I.T, Unconditional Love, Eastenders, This Is Personal, Insiders, Holby City, Inspector Lynley Mysteries, Gypsy Girl, Burnside.*

Film includes *London Road, The Broken, Cash Back, Left Turn.*

Charlie Young | Deputy Stage Manager
Charlie has been the Resident Stage Manager for Up In Arms since 2013. With Up In Arms: *Eventide* (Arcola and tour), *Visitors* (Bush Theatre, Arcola and tour), *Fear Of Music* (tour with Out of Joint).

Other theatre includes: *The Snail and the Whale, Emily Brown and the Thing, The Snow Dragon* (Tall Stories); *The Tiger Who Came To Tea* (Nick Brooke Productions Ltd.); *Garden* (Pleasance Courtyard); *Miss Caledonia* (House); *Barbican Box* (Barbican); *Hag, The Girl With The Iron Claws* (The Wrong Crowd); *The Idylls of the King* (Oxford Playhouse); *Pinocchio* (Berry Theatre); *Jesus Christ Superstar* (Ljubljana Festival, Slovenia); *The Hairy Ape, Antigone* (Southwark Playhouse); *Third Floor* (Trafalgar Studios); *Much Ado About Nothing, Twelfth Night* (Ludlow Festival).

GERMAN SKERRIES

Robert Holman

This edition is for David Eldridge.
Thank you for your friendship.

5

German Skerries was first presented at the Bush Theatre, London, on 25 January 1977, with the following cast:

JACK WILLIAMS	Paul Copley
MARTIN JONES	John Normington
MICHAEL HADDAWAY	Mark Penfold
CAROL WILLIAMS	Caroline Hutchison

Director	Chris Parr
Designer	Miki van Zwanenberg
Lighting Designer	Buz Williams

Characters

MARTIN JONES, *fifty-nine*
JACK WILLIAMS, *twenty-three*
MICHAEL HADDAWAY, *thirty-four*
CAROL WILLIAMS, *twenty-three*

The play takes place on an area of rough land known as South Gare at the entrance of the River Tees. South Gare juts out into the North Sea.

The Present Day

SCENE ONE
Friday 22 July

SCENE TWO
Saturday 23 July

SCENE THREE
Monday 8 August

Scene One

*Grass, one or two stones, and some half-bricks from a low wall
which is falling down. Near the wall is a wooden hut: painted on
the door in white lettering, 'Teesside Bird Club', and scrawled
down one side in aerosol paint, 'Boro Boot Boys Rule' and 'Jack
Charlton for Prime Minister'. An electricity cable runs through
the air to the hut. Resting against the other side are two oars.
Propped by the wall is an old battered rowing boat.*

July 22nd. A hot, humid, sticky afternoon.

JACK WILLIAMS *is sitting on the grass. He is twenty-three
and is wearing dirty jeans, a white T-shirt and ICI working
boots. He is a small, lightly built man. Beside him is a copy of*
The Hamlyn Guide to Birds of Britain and Europe, *a pair of
binoculars, a notepad and a bag of Fox's Glacier Fruits. He is
looking out to sea through his telescope.*

Behind him, beside the hut, is MARTIN JONES. *He is fifty-nine
and wearing a dark, baggy suit. He too is lightly built. He is
resting a ladies' bike against the hut.*

JACK *lowers his telescope for a moment. They see each other.*
JACK *nods shyly.*

MARTIN. Hello.

> JACK *looks through his telescope.* MARTIN *takes off his
> cycle clips and opens the saddlebag. He takes out an
> inflatable cushion and a pair of binoculars, puts the clips
> inside, and fastens it. The cushion and binoculars are on the
> ground.* MARTIN *stands for a moment.* JACK *lowers his
> telescope.*

Much about this afternoon?

JACK. Not a lot like.

MARTIN. It must be the weather that's to blame. The fine
weather.

JACK. It's a dead loss.

MARTIN stands for a moment. JACK puts his telescope on the grass. MARTIN takes a Yale key from his pocket and tries to open the hut door. JACK watches him. Eventually the door opens. MARTIN pushes his bike inside. He comes out and closes the door.

MARTIN. I always have the same trouble. I think it's those young hoodlums. (*Walking forward.*) Trying to get in and whatnot. I wish they'd leave the hut alone.

He is standing beside JACK.

Have you been here long?

JACK. 'Bout an hour.

MARTIN walks back to the door and picks up the binoculars and cushion.

(*Pointing out to sea.*) I've bin watchin' that ship.

MARTIN (*walking back*). Yes, I can see it. It will be waiting for the tide.

JACK. Reckon so?

MARTIN. Yes.

JACK. I've seen yer bike before like. A've alwez wondered 'oose it was.

MARTIN. Well it seems silly sometimes, it's safe in the hut. I don't walk very far, I'm more of a sitting-down man.

JACK. Yeah.

MARTIN. If nobody's inside –

A slight pause.

JACK. What's yer name?

MARTIN. Martin.

JACK. Jack or John, dependin' which yer prefer. Yer not on the committee like?

MARTIN. No.

JACK. Yer not a snob then.

MARTIN. No, I'm a common-or-garden me.

JACK. Jus' wondered – seein' yer y'know. Yer don' get many down on the Gare on a Fridi. People goyn out an' that, f'the evenin'.

MARTIN. The birdwatching hasn't been very good.

JACK. A thought it might 'ave been your duty.

MARTIN. I'm not very active on that side of the club. I don't know who is on today.

JACK. No like?

MARTIN. I'm glad – let other people get on with it. The world is full of other people who want to. I think you feel like me.

JACK. A'm alwez gettin' the wrong impression.

MARTIN. Not to worry.

> MARTIN *puts his cushion on the grass.* JACK *looks out to sea.*

JACK. 'E is bloody good, the captain o'that ship.

> MARTIN *puts his binoculars round his neck.*

MARTIN. What's he been getting up to?

JACK. Look a'that – the way 'e keeps it still in the water.

> MARTIN *looks through his binoculars for a brief moment.*

One o'the crew keeps runnin' up an' down the side. (*Looking through his telescope.*) I keep thinkin' o'that joke – 'opin' 'e'll throw somethin' over – and 'ave it come flyin' back.

MARTIN (*smiling*). Has he?

JACK. No – a don't give up though. I'm tryin' a'put the thought in 'is mind.

MARTIN. Why that? What about the poor sailor?

JACK (*still looking through his telescope*). It'd be a laugh. 'E's not gonna do it.

JACK *lowers his telescope.* MARTIN *picks up his cushion and starts to blow it up.*

Yer should see some of them foreigners down the docks. In the pubs. Puttin' funny things in their beer. I drink Tartan mesel' like – what they put in that would frighten yer. Blackcurrant and all bloody sorts.

MARTIN *holds the nozzle to stop the air coming out.*

MARTIN. That's not very kind of you.

JACK (*thinking*). I'n it?

MARTIN *blows another lungfull of air into the cushion.*

With all them. Spaniards and Poles, yer can't get in some nights.

MARTIN *fastens the cushion.*

Not that I go anyway like – they're so bloody rowdy – yer tekk yer life in yer hands.

MARTIN. Well then.

JACK. Every evenin' ends in a fight down there.

MARTIN *puts his cushion on the grass.*

All the biggest coppers roamin' about at 'alf past ten.

MARTIN (*sitting down*). My legs are tired. D'you come here often, Jack?

JACK. Now'n agen like.

MARTIN. I do too.

JACK. It's good, isn't it?

MARTIN. Yes, it is. It's very peaceful. It's not very often I meet someone.

JACK. No like?

MARTIN. It is possible to wander on your own, which is what I like doing.

JACK (*shyly*). Yes.

A foghorn sounds from the distance.

(*Looking out to sea.*) There she is – shiz movin'.

MARTIN *looks out to sea.* JACK *picks up his telescope and looks through it.*

There's that bloke agen.

MARTIN *looks through his binoculars.*

See 'im? (*Passing the telescope to* MARTIN.) 'Ere, yer'll get a better view with this.

MARTIN *looks through the telescope.*

MARTIN. He's the pilot. (*After a moment's pause.*) If you look the other side you can see a tug coming round.

JACK *looks through his binoculars.*

JACK. Eh, yer can.

MARTIN. Now can you see the cable?

JACK. Yeah.

MARTIN. The tug will tow it in.

JACK. Bloody great.

A slight pause.

'E 'as to work for 'is money that guy – there 'e is agen. (*After a moment's pause. Excited.*) Someone's with 'im this time.

The foghorn sounds from the distance.

That'll be the captain like?

MARTIN *lowers the telescope.*

MARTIN. I think the captain will be on the bridge.

JACK (*still looking*). Yer reckon?

A slight pause.

Shiz movin' anyway.

MARTIN. It's a Russian boat.

JACK (*to himself*). Great.

MARTIN. Here, have this. I've seen what I wanted to see.

JACK *takes the telescope, he looks through it*.

JACK. Ta.

MARTIN. It's a very careful operation bringing a boat that size in.

JACK. D'yer know all about this?

MARTIN. I've a friend who used to be a pilot.

JACK. Yeah?

A slight pause.

MARTIN. D'you know about the German Skerries?

The foghorn sounds, very loud.

JACK (*excited*). Look a'that, thess another tug comin' round! Fantastic!

MARTIN. Can you see those rocks to your left? They're the German Skerries.

The foghorn sounds, very loud. JACK looks to his left.

JACK. Yeah, I can.

MARTIN. At high tide you can just see the tip of them. The pilot has to steer clear.

A foghorn sounds, very loudly.

JACK. I can see 'em now.

MARTIN. At low tide you can see them far better.

JACK looks back to the ship.

That's why Teesmouth is very dangerous – because of those rocks bang in the middle.

JACK (*excited*). Yer wouldn't believe it, would yer? Look a'the cables.

MARTIN *raises and looks through his binoculars for a brief moment*.

If one a'those snapped someone'd get it. A wouldn't like it t'
be me.

MARTIN (*smiling*). The captain doesn't know he has an
audience.

JACK. You wouldn't think it, would yer?

MARTIN. What's that?

JACK. That two little tugs could pull a bloody great thing like
that.

MARTIN *smiles. The foghorn sounds, more quietly. A slight
pause.*

It's comin' up to those rocks.

He watches through his telescope in silence. MARTIN *walks
to the hut door and tries to open it with his key. Again he has
difficulty. The door opens. The sound of a flute. It runs up
through a scale. Sudden, short and snappy. Like the sound of
a bird soaring into the sky.*

JACK *moves quickly. He flops onto his back. With his feet in
the air he makes a 'V' shape by crossing his ankles. The end
of the telescope rests in this. He is like this for a split second.*

Cormorant.

*The cormorant flies above his head. He does a backward
roll, ends in a standing position, his telescope still on the
bird.*

(*Excited.*) Look at it go.

MARTIN *stumbles back to his binoculars, picks them up and
looks. He finds the bird.*

Cormorant. Look a'that.

A pause.

It's a divin'. I'nt it beautiful.

A pause.

It's bombin' the water. Look at it swoop.

MARTIN. There's no man on earth could do that.

A pause.

JACK. Oh man, look a'that – it's caught a bloody eel!

A slight pause.

MARTIN. It's a piece of wire.

JACK (*anxious*). What's it doin'?

MARTIN. It's a piece of wire, it's got it fast in its stomach.

A slight pause.

JACK. Where'd it get that from?

MARTIN. When it dived.

JACK (*quietly*). Poor bugger.

MARTIN *moves quickly to his left, following the bird. He nearly stumbles over.*

MARTIN (*excited*). There it goes, it's shaken it free.

JACK *follows it. They watch in silence for a moment.*

JACK. It's landed on the German Skerries.

The sound of the foghorn, quietly. A slight pause.

The boats crossin' 'em now.

A slight pause.

MARTIN. Look how it's ruffling its feathers. It must be hurt.

He lowers his binoculars and walks to the hut. The door is still open. JACK *is watching the cormorant.*

JACK. It's alright though.

MARTIN *takes a Thermos flask from his saddlebag. He leaves the door open.*

MARTIN. I've a flask of coffee. Would you like some?

JACK *lowers his telescope.*

JACK. No ta.

MARTIN. It makes me very angry. When I see something like that.

JACK. Yeah.

He sits down as before. MARTIN *is standing by his cushion, he pours himself coffee.*

MARTIN. It makes me angry.

JACK. Yeah like.

MARTIN *puts the cup carefully on the grass and screws the cap on the flask. He puts the flask down and picks up his cup.* JACK *looks at his watch.*

Would you 'ave the right time?

MARTIN *looks at his watch.*

MARTIN. Two minutes to four.

JACK. I can never tell with my watch. It says twenty past one at the moment.

MARTIN. I've had mine a long time.

JACK. So 'ave I like, that's the trouble.

MARTIN *smiles and sips his coffee.*

Si' down then.

MARTIN *puts his cup carefully on the grass.*

MARTIN (*sitting down*). I like the summer. When we have a summer it makes a pleasant change from winter.

He settles on his cushion.

Whereabouts d'you live, Jack?

JACK. Me like? Thornaby. Near what used t'be the railway line.

MARTIN. How d'you get there?

JACK (*pointing*). See that old Austin Healey Sprite wi' the dent in the bumper. The little green two-seater. That's mine. F'what it's worth – bits keep on droppin off it. 'Ump-back bridges're fatal.

MARTIN *smiles and sips his coffee*.

Yer guaranteed t'lose 'alf the sub-frame. Usually a lose the person next t'me an' all. A wanted a sports car like so a got one.

MARTIN. Yes.

JACK. I'm stupid, I suppose, but – yer can't account f' things people do 'alf the time like, so why should I account f' mesell. At the time I couldn't afford it, so I got it.

MARTIN. Whereabouts d'you work?

JACK. ICI Wilton.

MARTIN. Am I being nosey?

JACK. A' yer?

MARTIN. I'm a teacher. I teach in a primary school.

JACK. Pannel Man on't Cracker Plant me.

MARTIN. I teach in Redcar.

JACK. Very nice.

MARTIN. I have the top class – boys and girls of nine and ten.

JACK. Yes – a couldn't do that, they'd bash me up.

MARTIN. No they wouldn't.

JACK. You 'aven't seen 'em like – I suppose you 'ave.

MARTIN. I don't talk to an empty classroom.

JACK. No like – mekk meself sound stupid. Keep me mouth shut, shouldn' I?

MARTIN. Not at all.

JACK. I'll 'ave t'be off soon anyway.

MARTIN *sips his coffee*.

Jus' finished six till two, that's 'ow come I'm 'ere.

MARTIN *sips his coffee*.

MARTIN (*smiling*). My wife has sent me out from under her feet.

JACK. Oh aye?

MARTIN. She's busy packing. We're going on holiday. I put what I could into the car before coming out.

JACK. Good f' yer like.

MARTIN *sips his coffee.*

MARTIN. We're going to South Devon, to a place called Salcombe, I don't know whether you know it? It's a nice little spot.

JACK. A don't.

MARTIN. More and more people seem to. It's the sort of place you tell people about hoping they won't go, and the next thing, there they are walking down the main street.

JACK. Yes.

MARTIN. And we might as well have stayed at home. I don't mean that of course.

He sips his coffee.

I broke up from school at lunchtime. Ann's been at it all day.

He sips his coffee.

What I started out to tell you, was not to marry a girl with big feet.

JACK. I am married like.

MARTIN. I was going to tell you because it can be painful when you get under them, but obviously you know.

He smiles and shakes his head.

My class are always talking about *Star Trek* – back at home I wish Captain Kirk'd come and teleport me.

JACK *smiles.* MARTIN *sips his coffee.*

You wouldn't think there could be so much fuss over two weeks away. And it gets worse every year, Jack. I think she looks forward more to the fuss than the actual holiday. What do you do with a woman like that? If she were a child you'd buy her a spinning top and tell her to be quiet.

JACK *smiles*.

Don't smile.

JACK (*worried*). I –

MARTIN. I'm sorry, I was only joking.

JACK. A thought yer weren't.

MARTIN. I can see the amusing side.

The sound of the foghorn, very faintly.

I frightened you, didn't I?

JACK. Yer did a bit like.

MARTIN. I am sorry. Oh dear, I am sorry. I'm in need of a rest. Especially on the last day of term when the class are very excited and everything – they're quite a handful.

MARTIN *puts the cup on the grass*.

JACK. We're 'avin' the middle weeks of August.

MARTIN *stands, picks up his flask and puts it on the grass by the hut door. He walks back and sits down.*

MARTIN (*brightly*). Where are you going?

JACK. Don't know yet like. Somewhere.

MARTIN. Salcombe is a lovely spot.

He throws the dregs of his coffee from the cup onto the grass.

I'd always thought that would be the first signs of old age, going to the same place year after year. But we like it and it doesn't matter.

JACK *smiles*.

JACK (*leaning back, his elbow on the grass*). I 'aven't booked, I suppose I should 'ave done really. We have a mortgage y'see like an' don' wanna put off payin' it – not that a could if a wanted to.

MARTIN. That's the trouble, isn't it.

JACK. It is like, yer dead right. End up goyn somewhere f' the weekend probably. Trouble is we 'ad a 'oneymoon in January. We were goyn up to Scotland skiin' but there wasn' any snow so we ended up in Carlisle. Put the kibosh on that.

MARTIN *takes a white hanky from his pocket.* JACK *lies back on the grass.*

What's it like then Salcombe?

MARTIN (*mopping his brow*). It's a little fishing and boating town – getting slightly more spoilt, but it's still very peaceful – and holiday town of course. We stay on a houseboat.

JACK *puts his hands behind his head.*

JACK. Aren't yer leavin' it a bit late? T'be settin' off today?

MARTIN *shifts position slightly so that he is facing* JACK.

MARTIN. No, we travel down overnight.

He puts away his hanky.

We always have done. It made the journey more of an adventure. When the boys were little. It was the sort of thing we got in to. And we've carried on ever since.

He takes off his jacket, stands, picks up the cup and walks to the hut. He hangs his jacket on a nail and screws the cup onto the flask. JACK *watches him.*

The traffic was a lot quieter then.

He puts the flask by the hut door.

It was quite an unusual way to travel.

JACK. Yer must be nuts. It's miles and miles.

MARTIN *is still by the door, he turns to* JACK *and smiles.*

MARTIN. Thank you for that kind comment.

JACK. I didn't mean t'say that.

MARTIN (*walking back*). That's what my pupils say to me – I'll let you off this once.

JACK *sits up.*

JACK (*worried*). I –

MARTIN (*stopping him*). Never – regret anything in this life.
(*Smiling.*) Except marrying a nagging wife – I hold to that.

He sits down.

And another thing. Never take anything too seriously.

JACK (*leaning back*). Yer talk about yer wife, yer fuss about a
bit yersel like – (*Realising.*) I' m off agen, aren't a.

MARTIN (*smiling*). It's the years of training, Jack.

JACK *puts his hands behind his head.*

JACK (*almost flippant*). Sorry like.

MARTIN (*smiling*). Sorry, my left foot. (*More seriously.*) I
imagine the real boating people of Salcombe think we look
foolish because neither of us can swim and we wear those
yellow lifejackets. We stand out a mile as amateurs.

JACK. Yeah?

MARTIN. The houseboat is anchored in a place called The Bag
– moored, I should say really. Salcombe is on the mouth of
an estuary.

A slight pause.

Coming back we break the journey at my son's in
Gloucester. He's the Deputy Head of a large comprehensive
there – or rather one of two deputy heads, Martin's on the
teaching side. He's my eldest son. Stephen my other son
teaches in Romford.

The sound of the foghorn, very faintly. MARTIN *looks.*

Your boat is nearly in the docks.

The sound of a foghorn, loud. JACK *sits up.*

JACK. There's one comin' out look.

MICHAEL HADDAWAY *enters. He is thirty-four, has short
cropped hair, and is wearing wellingtons, fawn trousers, and
an Arran sweater. He is in a hurry, he is looking for
something.*

MICHAEL. Hello, Martin.

MARTIN. Hello, Captain Hook. (*Stumbling to his feet.*) How are you, Michael?

MICHAEL. My clock's still ticking but that's about it.

He sees the oars and goes to them.

I left these here so I wouldn't forget where they were and I've been looking for them f' half an hour. (*He is still.*) How're you? – long time no see.

MARTIN. One thing and another has kept me busy.

MICHAEL (*leaning against the side of the hut*). Yes? – musn't grumble?

MARTIN. No.

A slight pause.

MICHAEL. Neither must any of us, Martin.

MARTIN. How is Sheila?

MICHAEL. Very well, bearing up.

MARTIN. And the children?

MICHAEL. Bearing up too.

He takes a packet of Benson & Hedges from his pocket.

We're in the process of buying Lucy a pony, if we can find a field. James wants to take up hang-gliding.

He lights his cigarette.

Which is ridiculous for a ten-year-old. Apart from that life goes on as normal – never ask about my marriage, Martin. How's the other Martin?

MARTIN. Fine. We're seeing them in a fortnight. They're going to Greece on holiday shortly after.

JACK *is looking through his binoculars, scanning the horizon.*

MICHAEL (*still leaning against the hut*). Remember me to them.

MARTIN. I will do.

A slight pause.

How is it with you and Sheila?

MICHAEL. We've patched over the last quarrel. There are times when our marriage leaves little time for anything else. We both need to hang on to it – for the children's sake as well as our own – the children are old enough to cope now. We need to hang on to things, Martin, even though doing so is pretty hopeless.

MARTIN. Yes.

MICHAEL. I can't see her point of view. She can't see mine. Sheila sees our friends as being perfect matches, she thinks it's just us, James is in the middle with his Meccano set, Lucy with her pony. We're all concerned with our own little lot, Martin. All of it very stupid, none of it making sense.

He gathers up the oars.

I work twice as hard as a result.

JACK *lowers his binoculars.*

MARTIN. Yes.

MICHAEL (*brightly*). And remember me to Mrs Martin.

MARTIN. Ann.

MICHAEL. Yes.

MARTIN. I will do.

JACK *has taken a packet of twenty No6 from his pocket.*

MICHAEL (*walking towards* MARTIN). I've to row out to the Skerries.

Faintly from the distance, the bugle-like call of a herring gull.

(*Standing beside* MARTIN. *Hushed voice.*) I'm working for British Steel, you've never seen such a mess in all your born days.

JACK *lights a cigarette with a Zippo lighter.*

For a nationalised industry it speaks novels. (*Walking away.*)
Luckily I'm being paid. (*Walking back. Hushed voice.*) They
keep bringing men up from London – the first stage is
supposed to open on Tuesday – they haven't a clue, not an
iota of knowing what the job's about. They've got to get the
plant working and they don't know how to do it. (*Speaking
quickly, aggressively.*) They're having me out all hours of the
night. (*Walking away.*) Anyway, see you.

JACK *is watching.*

MARTIN. Cheerio, Michael.

MICHAEL (*hurrying*). I found my oars.

MICHAEL *has gone.* MARTIN *stands for a moment.* JACK
is looking at him.

MARTIN. My friend the pilot. He has his own business now,
running cargo to and from the rigs, and doing odd boating
jobs about the harbour. He's always in a hurry.

JACK. Yeah.

He puts the cigarettes and lighter back in his pocket.
MARTIN *walks to the hut door, goes inside and returns,
carrying a hard-backed notebook, the club sightings book. It
has a pen attached to it with string.*

*Very faintly, very gently, the sound of the sea can be heard
breaking against the shore. This remains until the end of the
scene.*

MARTIN (*to himself as much as to* JACK). Oh dear, it's a rum
old world. It's Sheila I feel sorry for.

*He picks up the flask, unscrews the cup and pours himself
coffee.* JACK *picks up his binoculars and looks inland.*
MARTIN *puts the flask by the door and returns to his
cushion, carrying the bird book and his coffee. He sits down
and sips.*

JACK. It don't seem real? Know what a mean?

He lowers his binoculars.

Watchin' them blokes like, buildin' the steel plant. It looks
like a ware'ouse.

MARTIN. It looks like a monstrosity.

JACK. An' wi' all that fencin' round the outside. (*It occurs to him*.) It looks like Colditz.

MARTIN. Yes. That's to stop the vandals getting in.

JACK. Stop blokes pinchin' stuff an' all, more like.

JACK looks through his binoculars at the steel plant.

It's gonna be massive.

MARTIN sips his coffee.

Bloody great cooling towers? Cool sommat they will.

JACK lowers his binoculars.

(*Leaning back on the grass.*) Sod me, it's gettin' hotter.

He puts one hand over his eyes.

Sun's bright.

He smokes. MARTIN *sips his coffee.*

I could jus' sail away on of them boats.

MARTIN. I thought you said you didn't like foreigners.

JACK (*sitting up*). A didn't say that.

He stubs his cigarette out on the grass.

Can't smoke when it's hot.

He leans back again. MARTIN *sips his coffee.*

Chuggin' along like, on the watery water.

MARTIN *places his cup carefully on the grass. He loosens his tie and undoes the top two buttons of his shirt.*

When I was a kid, I 'ad this dream. T'put all me stuff in a JCB an' drive off. Roamin' thee 'ole world. All I 'ad t'do was put a clean shirt in the scoop. Sounds daft dun it?

MARTIN. Yes.

JACK. Yeah, it does – a were a daft kid. That's all me ma ever bloody told me. Me dad thought a were bonkers. 'E's never 'ad an ambition in 'is life. 'E didn't know what a meant.

MARTIN *picks up his cup and takes a sip of coffee.*

You know what I'm gonna tell my kiddies? (*Thinking.*) About ambition? (*Thinking.*) You see, it doesn' matter if you do anythin' about yer ambition, so long as you've 'ad 'em. Then you've always got something to think about. (*After a moment's pause.*) I suppose that's true.

He raises his hand and looks at MARTIN *for a brief moment.*

MARTIN. Most of us are lazy and afraid, Jack. We don't do what our instincts tell us.

JACK (*shielding his eyes again*). What's that mean?

MARTIN. Sometimes we make a wrong choice. We forget what is important.

JACK (*getting bored with the conversation*). What is important like?

MARTIN. I've lived a few more years than you and I still don't know.

JACK. Nobody does, I reckon.

MARTIN *sips his coffee.*

MARTIN. Perhaps that's what I'm trying to say.

He takes a sip of coffee and then puts the cup carefully on the grass.

(*Undoing his shirt-sleeve buttons.*) When I was your age my instincts told me I should get up and leave the area. My mum and dad begged me to stay, so I did. Through no fault of their own they were short-sighted.

He picks up his coffee and takes a sip.

I remember my mother pawning her wedding ring to buy us shoes. She was determined that we should have a good education. It was a few years later, when they got older, that they became fuddy in their attitudes. Then out of a sense of responsibility I didn't feel I could let them down.

A slight pause.

Teach your children to ignore their sense of responsibility.
Teach them to love you. They're not the same thing.

JACK *raises his hand and looks at* MARTIN *for a brief
moment.* MARTIN *smiles.* JACK *sits up.* MARTIN *looks
through the bird book.*

There hasn't been a rare bird sighted for three weeks. Mr
Modley saw a puffin on June the twentieth.

JACK *stands up.*

JACK. Ground's 'ard. (*Picking up the bag of Glacier Fruits.*)
Want one o' these?

He offers the bag. MARTIN *takes one.*

What d'yer teach your classes?

*Faintly from the distance, the bugle-like call of a herring
gull.*

JACK *takes a sweet.*

MARTIN *puts his wrapper in his pocket,* JACK *throws his
away.*

MARTIN. A little bit of everything, Jack. I've tried to interest
them in birdwatching – occasionally one of them will come
to me and say they've seen a so-and-so and what is it. The
girls enjoy looking after the bird table. Apart from that
they're not very bothered.

JACK. ICI ain' much cop really. I've applied to go on a course
like – Carol keeps persuadin' me – f' promotion an' more
money an' that. A won't get it though, I never do.

MARTIN. Why not?

JACK. I dunno, I jus' don't.

MARTIN. Be an optimist.

JACK. Then I'd 'ave my 'ead in the clouds, wouldn' I? I won't
get it.

MARTIN. What's the course for?

JACK. It's a technical course like. Leads yer on t'bein' a plant
manager. Eventually like. ICI's daft – yer think it's great when
yer first start, cos there's never owt t'do. Yer can get by doin'
two hours' work in an eight-hour shift. Rest o'the time yer
playin' cards. Or dominoes. Or darts. Or shuv'apenny on the
control box – bloody daft – when yer reckon up the money
that must be wasted. The bosses've got their 'eads on the
wrong way. Not that there is anythin' fo'yer t'do like, yer jus'
see it's kept runnin'. If anything does go wrong and yer can't
'andle it, yer call in the supervisor – that's what I wanna be.
Mind, we're alright, we've got a good Union man – 'e int bin
bribed yet. 'Alf the shop stewards 'ave bloody posh 'ouses.
ICI were tryin' a lay men off our shift – they reckoned it was
overstaffed. The Unions wouldn't let 'em, thank God.

MARTIN *is listening to him. He throws the dregs of his*
coffee onto the grass.

We've a right idiot on our shift. Bloody good mind, 'e'll do
owt. He stands on 'is 'ead and tells jokes. Every Fridi night
'e tekks off 'is trousers an' runs round the block where 'e
lives. 'E's forty-three. 'E sez 'e does it to stir the
housewives. 'E's a Ccommunist. 'E's been to Russia twice.
Once wi' the Union and once on 'oliday. When yer talk to
'im properly 'e's some bloody good things to say. Yer know
'e sez all this about layin' men off is just an excuse, they
think they can do it now an' get away with it – because of the
economic trouble. He told us to stick to our guns. Which we
did like and won – I 'eard this mornin'.

MARTIN. I don't know, Jack, there's no rhyme or reason for a
lot of things.

JACK (*smiling*). It's not s'bad though eh?

MARTIN *stumbles to his feet.*

MARTIN. No. We're being told there is a depression, I don't
see much of it about. I try to understand what I can. (*Walking*
to the hut door.) When I tap my brain it doesn't always come
up with an answer. (*Bending down to pick up the flask.*) The
wheels have got rusty. (*Straightening up.*) Do people think
about these problems, Jack?

JACK. Suppose you 'ave to, don't yer?

MARTIN (*screwing the cup on the flask*). My next-door neighbour thinks about his roses.

He puts the flask by the hut door.

I often wonder why we have to be concerned with the way we all live – I don't know why we just don't get on with it. (*Walking back to his cushion.*)

MARTIN *is standing beside* JACK.

The sound of a foghorn, loud.

Both look out to sea.

There's a boat going out.

He takes his hanky from his pocket.

It's a Norwegian boat by the look of it.

He mops the sweat from his brow.

It'll've been carrying wood.

The sound of the foghorn, loud.

JACK. It's crossin' the German Skerries.

MARTIN *puts away his hanky and looks at the sky.*

MARTIN. I think the weather's going to break.

JACK *sits down, he looks briefly at his watch before remembering. He starts to pack his belongings up.*

JACK. Why're they called the German Skerries?

MARTIN. The German Skerries? I'm not sure exactly. In the Second World War when the Luftwaffe were bombing this area – you won't remember this, Jack, but there used to be a lot of gun emplacements along the shore, one of the planes they shot down crashed into the rocks. Skerries means rocks.

MARTIN *picks up his cushion and walks back to the hut. He puts his jacket over his arm and picks up his flask. He walks back to* JACK.

They were bombing the steel. And ICI.

A slight pause.

It'll be in an archive somewhere.

A siren from the steel plant sounds continuously.

JACK. They're knockin' off at the steel plant.

MARTIN (*looking at his watch*). Half past four. (*Offering his hand.*)

Thank you very much.

JACK *is taken aback. They shake hands.*

JACK. I've got to go an' pick up Carol.

MARTIN. I'm going for a walk.

JACK *exists.* MARTIN *watches him go.*

A slight pause.

MARTIN *picks up the sweet paper that* JACK *threw down earlier. He looks at the graffiti, slams the hut door closed and moves to exit.*

The sound of the sea fades up.

The lights fade to blackout.

Scene Two

The sound of the sea pounding against the shore.

A maroon goes off, it is very loud, the sound splinters and echoes.

Fifteen seconds' pause. A maroon, as before. Fifteen seconds' pause. A third maroon.

Lights pull up:

Saturday, July 23rd, eleven o'clock at night. The weather has broken, the air is damp, a slight storm is blowing.

JACK *and* CAROL WILLIAMS *standing together.* JACK *is wearing a brown pinstriped suit. His tie is loose round his neck.*

CAROL *is twenty-three, slightly smaller than* JACK, *thin and blonde. She is wearing her best dress and shoes.*

JACK (*excited*). Look a'that, there it is, it's a flare – it's the lifeboat.

CAROL. Frightened me to death, it's spooky.

JACK. Sommat's 'appened somewhere.

CAROL. Give me the willies.

JACK. What?

CAROL. This place, never mind that.

JACK. It's alright.

He listens for a moment at the sea.

(*Hushed voice.*) Listen to tha'. I'nt it great?

The harsh cackling 'kwuririp' of a black-headed gull.

(*Hushed voice.*) I'n it fantastic. Remember when we used to come 'ere?

CAROL *smiles and puts her arm around his waist.*

CAROL. Yeah.

JACK. Wasn't s'long ago like.

CAROL. No.

JACK. Remember –

CAROL (*interrupting him*). Don't you get cheeky. It gave me the willies then, it still does now.

JACK. I don't remember you sayin' no.

CAROL (*putting her foot down*). What did I just say?

JACK. What did yer just say?

CAROL. You know very well.

JACK. No, I don't – I've got a lousy memory.

CAROL. It wasn't s'bad a moment ago – I'm cold.

JACK hugs her to him.

JACK (*whispering*). Less go inside the hut.

CAROL. Not on your life, once you get me in there.

JACK. It's been cleaned.

CAROL. 'Undreds of spiders, no.

JACK. Yer didn' mind before – it's bin kept clean by the snobs.

CAROL. I wish you wouldn't use that word.

JACK. What word?

CAROL. You know.

JACK (*whispering*). Come on then.

CAROL. What d'you keep whispering for?

JACK. There might be people about?

CAROL. Out 'ere? There's only us mad enough – I should 'ave said you, there's only you mad enough.

JACK. Thanks a bunch.

He tickles her.

CAROL. Stop that.

JACK stops.

I don't know what I 'ave t'do with you sometimes.

JACK. Come inside thee 'ut.

CAROL. Get lost – 'ow many times, John?

JACK (*whispering*). 'Ow many times what?

CAROL. D'you 'ave t'be told. Yer in a funny mood tonight.

JACK (*whispering*). I can't 'elp it.

CAROL. You can never 'elp anything.

JACK. It were the way a were brought up.

CAROL. Well you certainly didn't get it from me.

JACK. Liar. (*Whispering in her ear.*) Liar, liar, liar.

CAROL (*shivering*). I am cold.

JACK. Let's face the other way.

> *The harsh cackling 'kwuririp' of a black-headed gull.* JACK
> *and* CAROL *turn 180 degrees.*

Better?

CAROL. Yeah.

> JACK *pushes* CAROL *back round. They stand as before.*

I'll brain you.

> JACK *pushes* CAROL *round 180 degrees.*

JACK. Out of the wind.

CAROL. Yer a madman, you.

> *She shivers.*

Oh, let's go inside the hut then. I should 'ave brought me coat.

> JACK *marches to the hut door.*

JACK. Carol.

CAROL. What?

JACK. Yer me sweetheart.

CAROL. When you get your own way I am.

JACK opens the door with his key. He turns the electric light on.

Light floods out through the door and through various knotholes in the wood.

MARTIN*'s bike can be seen.*

JACK. 'E's left 'is bike. (*Turning to* CAROL.) That bloke a were tellin' yer about.

He picks a slip of paper up from the floor.

'E's left a note. (*Reading.*) Couldn't get the door open – daft codger.

JACK *puts the note on the bike's saddle.* CAROL *is standing by the door.*

CAROL. Let me in then.

JACK *comes out.* CAROL *walks in.* JACK *takes a packet of cigarettes from his jacket pocket.*

(*Slightly worried.*) There's a spider.

JACK *lights two cigarettes with his lighter, he gives one to* CAROL.

Let's go soon.

JACK *puts his cigarettes away. They both smoke.*

JACK. I'm slightly drunk.

CAROL. A thought yer were.

The bugle-like call of a herring gull followed by the 'kwuririp' of a black-headed gull. JACK *walks away from the hut.*

(*Standing in the doorway.*) Let's go soon.

The bugle-like call of a herring gull.

JACK. It's not the same, is it?

He looks towards the German Skerries.

CAROL. What a night to be out 'ere.

JACK. That old man said the weather would break.

CAROL. There's no moon.

JACK (*startled. He has seen something at the German Skerries*). Eh! Eh! Carol!

He looks worried.

CAROL. What's the matter?

JACK (*staring*). Can see sommat!

CAROL (*stepping out of the doorway*). What're you on about?

JACK. Over there – somethin's 'appenin'.

CAROL (*walking to him*). Where?

JACK. Over there on them rocks!

CAROL. What rocks?

The harsh cackling 'kwuririp' of a black-headed gull.

JACK (*frightened*). It's a German! It's a fuckin' German.

CAROL (*looking*). What are you on about?

JACK. Comin' out the water. See it?

CAROL (*taking him more seriously*). I can see something.

JACK. It is, it's a German.

CAROL. What German?

JACK. Climbin' onto the rocks – look!

CAROL. This is gettin' silly.

JACK. What we gonna do, Carol?

CAROL. Turn the light out, we'll see better.

JACK. I think we should bloody go.

CAROL. Don't be silly, there's got t'be an explanation.

CAROL *walks to the hut door.* JACK *is still staring towards the German Skerries.*

Where's the light switch?

JACK. By the door.

> CAROL *turns the light out. It is very dark, they can only vaguely be seen.*

> CAROL *walks back to* JACK.

> (*Slightly calmer.*) 'E's on the rocks, look. Thess a glow in the water.

CAROL. I alwez said this place was spooky.

JACK (*excited*). Look a'tha' glow! – thess a light in the water.

> CAROL *puts her arm round his waist.*

CAROL. What d'yer think it is?

JACK. It's movin', it's a bloody arc light!

> *The beam from a powerful arc light flits across them very quickly. It is dark again.*

> Someone's liftin' it out of the water.

CAROL. Why did you say it was a German?

JACK (*excited*). It's a bloody diver look! Can yer see 'im?

> *The beam of the arc light pulls back across them.*

> They're shinin' it at us.

> *The beam passes. It is dark again.*

CAROL. D' you think we ought to tell someone?

JACK. 'Oo do we tell.

CAROL. They could be doin' anythin'!

> *A gust of wind blows up.*

> (*Concerned.*) We must do something.

JACK (*calmer*). There's another diver look, there's two of 'em.

> *A gust of wind blows up.*

CAROL. Why did you say it was a German?

JACK. A story.

CAROL. Anythin' t'do with the war?

JACK (*doing a Nazi salute*). Heil moustache!

He marches for a moment, making explosion noises.

CAROL. Come 'ere, I don't like t'think of them out there.

JACK puts his arm round her waist.

A gust of wind blows up.

The harsh cackling 'kwuririp' of a black-headed gull.

JACK. Listen t'them gulls.

CAROL (*suddenly*). John, there's the lifeboat!

They watch for a moment.

JACK. It's tryin' a get near them rocks.

A slight pause.

One o'the divers has got a line.

A slight pause.

It can't a'been a boat 'it the rocks, we'd of seen it, it's low- tide.

CAROL. There is a boat look, a small one.

A slight pause.

JACK. I int seen anythin' like this since –

A slight pause.

A can't think of owt. Since your mam's face when she nearly caught us.

A slight pause.

CAROL. D'yer think we ought to tell the police?

A slight pause.

JACK. The divers are gettin' in the lifeboat.

A pause.

(*Whispering.*) Get yer knickers off then.

CAROL *ignores him*.

(*Whispering*.) Get yer knickers off.

A slight pause.

CAROL. 'Aven't you finished?

JACK (*cheekily*). No. I like yer with yer knickers off.

CAROL. Talk about the leopard changin' 'is spots.

JACK. I'm in love with yer.

CAROL. Don't think you can bribe me with that blackmail.

JACK. It's not blackmail, it's true.

CAROL. You wouldn't know what was true if it stood up to shake hands with yer.

JACK. Don't say that about me.

CAROL. What did we get married for?

JACK. I like yer with yer clothes on as well. Sometimes, anyway.

CAROL *smiles at him*.

Yer mekk me feel awful.

CAROL (*putting her arm round his waist*). I don't mean to.

JACK. Get 'em off then. (*Kisses her on the cheek*.) Cos I love yer.

He kisses her on the lips.

I'm feelin' like I want t'be loved.

CAROL. God, you are drunk.

JACK (*kissing her on the neck*). Knickers, knickers, knickers.

CAROL *smiles*.

Know what I think about you.

CAROL. Astound me.

JACK. I think you're wonderful. (*Kissing her neck*.) Second to Lilly Smithers 'oo I went out with when I was nine.

CAROL. Yer not s'daft you, a'yer?

JACK. I'm a brain surgeon.

CAROL. The first brain to look at is yours.

JACK (*kissing her on the lips*). Don't be like that.

He picks her up.

I'm goin' t'carry you across the threshold agen.

He puts her down.

CAROL. The first time you were so drunk you dropped me. I 'ad a big bruise on me bum f'weeks after.

JACK. Don't say that.

He kisses her.

CAROL. I don't know 'ow we ever got to Carlisle.

JACK. Love me.

He puts his arm round her waist. They are looking towards the German Skerries.

CAROL. The lifeboat's goyn.

A pause.

JACK (*more soberly*). If I 'adn't started comin' 'ere with you I'd a never got interested in birdwatching.

A slight pause.

If your mam 'ad known.

CAROL. Well she doesn't and still doesn't, I 'ope. That's the way I want t'keep it.

JACK. I might tell 'er. Give me some money an' I won't.

CAROL. Have my dad t'face?

JACK. I can stand up to 'im.

CAROL. You and whose army?

JACK. I could. I bet you were awful when you were at school bossin' the other girls about.

A slight pause.

Your mam doesn't like me.

CAROL. Course she does, it's just that yer never say anythin'.

JACK. A do.

CAROL. Yer don't – yer jus' sit there.

JACK. What am I supposed t'say? It's yer dad, 'e puts me off –
I open me mouth, then a change me mind. Cos he's lookin'
at me.

CAROL. Well don't let 'im.

JACK. 'Ow can a stop him? – he's starin'.

CAROL. That's his way of bein' friendly.

JACK. A believe that.

CAROL. It is. Stare back.

JACK. A've tried. A go to take a slice o'bread an' there 'e is
lookin' at me. A daren't ask f' the jam in case 'e kills me.

CAROL. Yer exaggeratin'.

JACK. I'm not. Ever since a first met 'im 'e's been like that.

CAROL. It's because 'e's in love with me.

JACK. Get off.

CAROL. I don't mean sexual. He hated our Arnold. That's why
Arnold joined the army.

JACK. Arnold?

CAROL. Yes.

JACK. 'Ow does that explain why 'e stares at me?

CAROL. It does.

JACK. I've never 'eard you say anthin' like this before.

CAROL. Let's forget about it – me dad doesn't matter.

JACK. 'E does t'me.

CAROL. Why should 'e? 'E's nothin' t'do with us.

JACK. Well 'e is when I'm round there. An' another thing I
don't like the way your mother calls me pet. I'm not 'er pet.

CAROL. She's bein' friendly.

JACK. Some friendly. I could see 'er workin' it all out at the weddin'.

CAROL. Don't stare at me dad, that's all. Me mam feels uncomfortable.

JACK. Your 'ouse is so small there's nowhere else to look.

CAROL. Look at the floor.

JACK. That's what a do. That's what yer tellin' me not to do.

CAROL. Yer arkward, you are.

JACK. I can't talk if I'm lookin' at the floor.

CAROL. Look at the ceiling then.

JACK. If a do that, yer dad thinks I'm criticisin' 'is handiwork – that big hole where Arnold put 'is foot through. A can't win.

A slight pause.

CAROL. Just be polite.

A slight pause.

JACK. I find it embarrassin' when she calls me pet.

CAROL. I 'ave told 'er not to do that.

JACK. Well tell 'er agen. Shiz thick, your mam.

CAROL. It's because Arnold is away in the army.

JACK. I'll bash Arnold next time I see 'im.

A slight pause.

CAROL. Me mam does like you yer know.

JACK. She has a funny way of showing it.

A slight pause.

CAROL. She likes 'er family. So does me dad deep in that stone-cold heart of his.

A slight pause.

You have to blame people for certain things, but not me dad.
Cos it's not his fault, being laid off twice in 'is life –

JACK (*interrupting her*). I know he's been laid off, I know he's
been ill. (*Pulling her close to him*.) I'm sorry if I went on a bit.

CAROL (*tenderly*). Just talk to them.

JACK. Throw a drownin' man two ends of a rope, you would.
(*Taking her hand*.) Come on, let's go.

The light in the hut goes on.

MICHAEL *is standing there. He is wearing a wetsuit and a
black oilskin and he is soaked from head to toe. He has an
arc light in his hand. He looks in pain.*

JACK *and* CAROL *jump, they are startled by the light.*

JACK (*turning round*). What –

MICHAEL. Could one of you help me? Could one of you take
this. I'm sorry, I –

JACK *helps him. He puts the arc light on the grass.*
MICHAEL *leans against the hut.*

CAROL. Are you alright?

MICHAEL. Yes.

CAROL (*going to him*). Yer don't look it.

MICHAEL (*pushing CAROL's hand away*). I'm fine, I can
manage.

A sudden twinge of pain hits his stomach, he bends double.

CAROL (*trying to*). Let me help you, yer daft thing.

MICHAEL (*pushing her hand away, straightening up. Angry*). I
can manage. Sorry, shouldn't snap, it's passing.

*A small trickle of blood is coming from one corner of
MICHAEL's mouth.*

(*Bending double, trying to speak*.) I – I –

CAROL *helps him, she puts her arm round his shoulder.*

CAROL (*to* JACK, *urgent*). Get the car.

JACK *starts to exit*.

MICHAEL (*straightening up*). Wait a minute.

CAROL (*to* MICHAEL). Don't be silly.

JACK (*walking back*). What 'appened, mate?

CAROL (*to* JACK). Get the car. (*To* MICHAEL.) Look, yer
bad, yer must let us help you.

JACK. What 'appened?

CAROL (*to* JACK). Give me yer 'anky.

JACK *gives* CAROL *his hanky*.

(*Wiping the blood from round* MICHAEL's *mouth*.) Yerve
cut yer mouth.

MICHAEL. I was workin' for British Steel. On the pipe that
leads to the German Skerries when it seemed to explode. My
rowing pram overturned.

CAROL *gives* JACK *his hanky. A little more blood trickles
from* MICHAEL's *mouth*.

Can you help me off with this? I didn't want to go in the
lifeboat.

CAROL *and* JACK *help him off with his oilskin*.

(*Smiling*.) I didn't think I was hurt very bad. That's better.

JACK *is holding the oilskin*.

CAROL. Get the car, John.

JACK. What do I do with this? – 'ere, you have it.

He gives CAROL *the oilskin and exits quickly*.

CAROL. 'E won't be a minute.

MICHAEL *unzips the front of his wetsuit. A faint red mark
can be seen on his stomach*.

MICHAEL. I'm a fool. (*Bending double, in agony*.) I – I'm a
fool.

CAROL *is getting flustered, she doesn't know what to do.*

CAROL (*putting her arm round his shoulder*). Don't worry.

MICHAEL *straightens up.*

MICHAEL. Can you get me sitting down.

CAROL *helps him sit down. She puts the oilskin on the grass beside him.*

That's better. That's better.

CAROL *puts the oilskin over his lap.*

CAROL (*to herself*). Come on, come on.

CAROL *runs her fingers through his hair.*

Don't worry.

MICHAEL*'s face is white.*

MICHAEL (*calmly, slowly*). Did you know? – I'm a Catholic.

A slight pause.

If I were a Jew or a Protestant it wouldn't make any difference.

CAROL. Please don't try and talk.

MICHAEL *is talking to himself.*

MICHAEL. You're supposed to know the answer, aren't you.

A slight pause.

When everything is put in its place.

CAROL *keeps looking anxiously for the car.*

A slight pause.

Well, at the end of the day I don't know any more than I did before.

The sound of a car pulling up.

A slight pause.

Once a Catholic, always a Catholic.

The sound of a car door opening.

CAROL. 'E's 'ere.

MICHAEL. I feel peaceful now.

> *He makes the movements of a man being sick. A clot of blood comes out of his mouth and onto the oilskin. CAROL's hands go in front of her face in horror, she nearly screams.*

(*Calmly.*) That's better. That was stuck in my throat.

CAROL (*putting her arm round his shoulder*). What's 'appenin'?

> JACK *enters.*

JACK. Right.

> CAROL *looks distressed.*

Everythin' okay?

CAROL (*trying to talk quietly*). 'E's 'urt 'is stomach inside.

JACK (*standing by* CAROL). I'll take 'im.

CAROL (*firmly*). I'm tekkin' 'im.

JACK (*talking quietly*). No, I will.

CAROL (*upset*). What am I gonna do then?

JACK. Stay 'ere.

CAROL. I'm not stayin' 'ere, I couldn't.

JACK. I won't be long.

CAROL. I've got to tekk him.

JACK. Why?

CAROL. I don't wanna stay 'ere.

JACK. It's the same f' me.

CAROL. If you 'adn't got that bloody sports car, I'm tekkin' 'im.

JACK. Where will yer go?

CAROL. Redcar.

JACK. What if it's shut?

CAROL. It'd be the same f' you, wouldn' it. 'Elp me get 'im up.

She still has her arm round MICHAEL*'s shoulder.* JACK *moves the oilskin from his lap. They stand him up.*

Take yer jacket off.

JACK *takes his jacket off. He puts it round* MICHAEL*'s shoulders.*

JACK (*whispering*). Are you sure?

CAROL. Yes. (*To* MICHAEL.) Can yer walk a bit?

MICHAEL. Yes.

JACK (*taking* MICHAEL*'s other arm*). Come on then.

They exit towards the car.

A pause.

The sound of a car door closing.

A pause.

The sound of the car pulling away.

A pause.

JACK *enters, he looks lost, he doesn't know what to do. The wind blows up.*

He pulls the oilskin round to the side of the hut out of the way. He stands looking towards the German Skerries.

The sound of a flute, the same notes as before.

A moment's pause.

The sound of the sea increases in volume. The wind blows up. It is very loud.

JACK *goes inside the hut, he closes the door.*

The sound stays for fifteen seconds and then slowly dies down as the lights pull up.

Early morning, five o'clock. The air is still. Absolute silence. A pause.

The silence is broken by the faint 'chug-chug' of a small fishing boat going out to sea and the sounds of the seagulls following it.

CAROL enters, she looks tired and drawn and has a car rug round her shoulders. She is carrying JACK's jacket over her arm.

CAROL. John. (*More loudly.*) John.

She taps on the hut door.

John. (*Knocking.*) John.

The hut door opens. CAROL has woken him from sleep. His hair is dishevelled and his tie is hanging from his trouser pocket.

The light in the hut is still on.

For a moment they look at each other.

JACK. Where've yer bin?

CAROL walks away a foot.

Sorry a spoke – yer didn' 'ave t' be this long.

CAROL walks back and gives him his jacket.

Ta – I've been wantin' a fag.

He puts on his jacket and takes the packet of cigarettes from his pocket.

Want one?

CAROL. Where were yer two hours ago?

JACK has the packet in his hand. He hasn't taken one.

The police came lookin' fo' yer.

JACK. I was 'ere.

CAROL. Asleep, I bet?

JACK. So?

CAROL (*breaking down*). 'E died, John, 'e died.

> CAROL *is in* JACK*'s arms.*

> Why weren't yer here?

> *She is sobbing.*

JACK. I was, love. Oh, love.

CAROL. I can't 'elp it.

> JACK *is holding her tightly.*

JACK. Sssh.

> *A pause.*

> JACK *manages to put the cigarettes back in his pocket.*

> Sssh.

> *A slight pause.*

> Sssh.

CAROL. 'E kept askin' me all sorts of questions. 'E kept tellin' me about 'is mistress an' stuff like that. I didn't know what to say.

> *A pause.*

> Then when a got 'im to the hospital an' they wheeled 'im in 'e was dead. They 'ad to fetch a priest. 'E kept askin' f' one. Then they left the priest wi' 'is body.

JACK. Sssh.

> CAROL *is still sobbing.*

> Sssh.

> *A pause.*

> I 'ad a walk around, love. I wen' an' ad a look at the new steel plant.

CAROL. 'E kept on callin' God a bastard.

> *A slight pause.*

> I've gone an' crashed the car an' all. Comin' back.

JACK. Sssh.

CAROL. Near the level crossing on Todpoint Road.

JACK. Sssh.

A slight pause.

'Ow bad is it?

CAROL. The front.

JACK. The front was bashed in anyway.

CAROL. Not like this.

JACK. It's alright.

CAROL. I 'ad to walk from the end of the Gare.

JACK. Are you alright?

CAROL. Yes – yer won't like it.

JACK. Listen, who do I care about, you or the car?

CAROL. Me.

JACK. Well then, I'm not gonna worry about the car, am I?

CAROL. No.

JACK. That's sense, isn't it?

CAROL. Yes.

JACK. Stand up a minute, I need a fag.

The fishing boat has gone. Silence.

CAROL *stands up.*

CAROL. I'm better.

She takes a hanky from his trousers pocket. JACK *takes out his cigarettes.* CAROL *sees the blood on the hanky.*

I don't want to use that.

She pushes the hanky back in his pocket.

JACK. I've got a clean one.

He takes a neatly folded clean hanky from his other pocket.
CAROL *dries her eyes with it.* JACK *lights a cigarette, he offers it to* CAROL.

CAROL. No thanks.

JACK puts his cigarettes and lighter away. He looks at his watch.

JACK. I don't know what time it is.

CAROL. Five o'clock. I know what to get you for your birthday.

She gives him the hanky. JACK *puts it in his jacket pocket.*

He puts his arm round her waist.

JACK. It's gettin' light.

He turns off the hut light, walks back and puts his arm round her waist again.

That's better, isn' it?

Silence. They stand there.

Cold?

CAROL. No, not really.

JACK. I am a bit.

Silence.

JACK pushes CAROL *forward, they walk a few steps.*

Silence.

CAROL. There's a pipe that runs from the river, to that steel plant, and back out to those rocks.

JACK. Mmm?

CAROL. What's the matter?

JACK. I was thinkin', love.

CAROL. What about?

JACK. I was lookin' at all that out there. What were yer sayin'?

CAROL. I don't know, I didn' understand it all. The pipe goyn t'the rocks is carryin' boiling hot water.

JACK. Who told yer this?

CAROL. People from the paper were at the hospital. It's goyn to affect the bird life.

JACK. It's what?

CAROL. The hot water. Millions of gallons a day comin' out by those rocks.

JACK. Say this agen?

CAROL. It'll affect the bird life.

JACK. What, love – there's a pipe from the river?

CAROL. So 'e told me.

JACK. I don't get this.

CAROL. The pipe from the river brings the water, it gets boiled, and then sent out there.

JACK. Why?

CAROL. How should I know, love.

A slight pause.

JACK. What else?

CAROL. A lot of things but I can't remember.

JACK. Try.

CAROL. Don't press me, John, I can't.

A slight pause.

It was low-tide last night. That's why they were down there. Tryin' to fix it. They'd two days. Part of the pipe gave way, exploded, and turned 'is boat over.

A slight pause.

The plant can't operate without the pipe.

JACK. I wish I'd got me telescope.

CAROL. I feel different this mornin'.

CAROL *shivers*.

JACK. Yer cold, we'll go in a minute.

CAROL. Where to?

JACK. Home.

CAROL. What in? There's no buses for hours.

JACK. Won't the car go at all?

CAROL. No. That's what I tried to tell yer.

JACK. We can phone a minicab.

CAROL. Walk to Redcar?

JACK. 'Ave you anythin' else you'd like to do?

   JACK *smiles*.

CAROL. No.

JACK. I bet you like anythin' that water cools a turbine.

CAROL (*shivering*). I'm freezing.

JACK. I bet you it does.

CAROL. 'Adn't we better set off then?

JACK. 'Ang on a minute. I bet you any money. Of course it
   does. It'll cool a steam turbine. You can see the cooling
   tower. It's like the ethylene plant I work on.

CAROL. I'm not very bothered at this moment.

JACK (*getting excited*). No listen –

   A slight pause.

   Any money on it. They'll be using the turbine to generate
   electricity. The turbine works on steam. It's a bit like a
   windmill, Carol. They 'ave t'cool the steam down so they
   take cold water from the river.

CAROL. Yer sound like a teacher.

JACK. It's like a car radiator. The water'll get bloody 'ot if it's
   coolin' that amount of steam. All the time. Day in day out.

Where they're going to pump the water out it'll raise the
temperature of the sea. It'll scare the birds on them rocks off.
(*Excited at working it out*.) Fuckin' 'ell. There'll be bloody
fireworks. Don't yer see what I mean, Carol? Are you feelin'
a bit better anyway, love?

He squeezes her.

I meant what I said las' night. I wasn't that drunk.

He stubs out his cigarette.

A slight pause.

I feel a bit sick. Not of you though, pet.

CAROL. Don't you start calling me pet.

JACK. I'm gettin' me own back on yer mam.

A slight pause.

CAROL. A do feel different, John. I've bin thinkin' a lot.

JACK. I know what you want.

CAROL. What?

JACK. You wan' us to settle down an' stop goyn out an' that.

CAROL. No a don't.

JACK. I don't want to. Not jus' yet.

CAROL. It's not that, John.

JACK. What is it then?

CAROL. I'm very proud o'you yer know.

JACK. What mekks yer feel different then?

CAROL. What's 'appened last night.

A slight pause.

JACK. When I've bin on that course an' got a new job we'll be
settled, won't we?

CAROL (*hugging him*). Oh, I do 'ope so.

JACK (*smiling*). Give over.

He picks up a small pebble and throws it into the air.

Catch.

He catches the pebble himself throws it up again, and kicks it with his foot.

Charlie Geroge. Should 'ave said Mills, shouldn' I? – if I'm supportin' Middlesbrough.

CAROL. I sometimes feel I'm pushin' you into things.

JACK (*walking away*). Lamp posts?

CAROL. You know what I mean.

JACK *picks up a pebble, he throws it into the air and uses the palm of his hand as a tennis racket.*

JACK. Björn Borg – no, not 'im, 'e's Swedish.

CAROL *picks up a pebble, she throws it at him.* JACK *kicks it away with his foot. He walks back to her.*

(*Holding up his crossed fingers.*) I've got me fingers crossed. An' me toes. I've got this feelin' inside o'me, that they're not gonna let me on it.

CAROL. Don't be silly.

JACK. I'm bein' serious.

Silence.

CAROL. Somethin' inside all of us. Yer mustn't think they won't let you.

JACK. I know that, but wi' me – I never 'ave that luck.

CAROL. It's not luck, get that out of your head, it's ability.

JACK. Ability to be lucky.

CAROL. Don't be sarcastic. (*Putting her arm round his.*) Why d'yer keep tellin' me I want to settle down? It's not true.

JACK (*smiling*). Sommat t' say.

CAROL (*smiling*). Yer not gettin' away with that. It isn't true.

JACK. A thought yer liked it when I fooled about?

CAROL. I do.

JACK. Well then, we're not gonna settle down, a'we?

CAROL. No.

JACK (*smiling*). Fat chance wi' me anyway.

CAROL (*smiling*). No.

JACK. No, what?

CAROL. A don't know.

JACK. Perky, pet?

CAROL. John.

JACK. Trouble is wi' me like, I wan' t'do allsorts.

CAROL. We can.

JACK. When yer look at all those lights. (*Points inland.*)

CAROL. What?

JACK. That's 'ow I imagine people will live on the Moon.
Little bases all over. Little blocks of light.

CAROL (*being silly*). D'you want to live on the Moon?

JACK. No, I'm only guessing like. I was jus' lookin' at it all.
When we're on 'oliday we'll 'ave to 'ave a walk up on Eston
Nab. When I was a kiddie we used t'climb up there an' one
way yer looked all yer could see was moors and fields, and
yer turned round and there was Teesside right down below
yer. We used t'play emperors – 'king of all I survey'. We
worked out what we would do if we ruled it.

*He walks and puts the arc light inside the hut. He looks at
the oilskin.*

What 'ave I t'do with this?

CAROL. Better put it inside 'adn' t we?

JACK *puts the oilskin inside the hut. He closes the door. He
picks up a pebble, throws it into the air, and lets it fall to the*

ground.

Dawn has come up a little more.

His wife was there last night.

JACK. Come'n stand where I am.

CAROL *goes and stands beside him. They are looking inland.*

Look a'that. A mass of industry. I've never seen it this time o'the mornin' before.

A slight pause.

Don't yer get the feelin' yer right in the middle of somethin'?

A slight pause.

(*Pointing from left to right.*) The lights o'Redcar. British Steel. ICI Wilton. Middlesbrough. The docks. Warners Chimney. Teesport refinery. The Transporter. ICI Billingham. Haverton Hill. Hartlepool. Stretches f' thirty miles. In the middle of it, we're 'ere. On a jut a'land. Fantastic. (*Shouting very loudly.*) HELLO, HELLO, HELLO.

(*After a moment's pause.*) Nobody can 'ear us.

The lights fade.

Scene Three

Lights snapped up.

Monday, August 8th, eleven o'clock in the morning. The day is overcast but warm.

From the steelworks, the faint sounds of a small crowd demonstrating.

CAROL *is standing on the grass, she is looking in the direction of the steelworks. She has a copy of* Travels with My Aunt *in her hand and is wearing a cardigan over her dress.*

MARTIN *enters, he looks very brown after his holiday and he is wearing the same suit. He strides towards the door.*

CAROL *looks at him for a moment.* MARTIN *takes a key from his pocket. He crosses his fingers.*

MARTIN (*to himself*). New key.

   The door opens easily, the arc light and oilskin have gone but the bike is still there.

   CAROL *sits down on the grass and opens her book.*

   The sound of the crowd fades to silence.

   MARTIN *wheels his bike from the shed, closes the door, and leans his bike against it.*

   CAROL *closes her book and puts it beside her on the grass. For a brief moment the faint sound of the crowd.*

   You look lost, my dear, is there anything I can do?

CAROL. No, I'm waitin' for my husband.

MARTIN. Whereabouts is he?

CAROL. Somewhere.

MARTIN. Is it as bad as all that?

CAROL (*standing up*). I expect 'e'll come carryin' 'is tail be'ind 'im with a list of excuses.

   She walks over to MARTIN.

MARTIN. Never mind. My tyres are flat. Is he a birdwatcher?

CAROL. Yes.

MARTIN. I thought so, I could tell by the moan.

CAROL. I think you know 'im.

MARTIN. Do I?

CAROL. You've jus' been on holiday.

MARTIN (*smiling*). Yes.

CAROL (*smiling*). I know all about you you see.

MARTIN (*smiling*). I think you know more about me than I do myself.

CAROL. His name's Jack.

MARTIN. Yes, yes, I remember.

CAROL. We found your note.

MARTIN. I thought it would blow away, the weather was looking so bad.

CAROL. I'm Carol.

MARTIN. Hello, Carol.

CAROL. 'Ello.

For a brief moment the faint sound of the crowd.

MARTIN *takes the pump off the bike.*

You got back yesterday?

MARTIN. Last night at ten o'clock. (*Taking the connecting pipe from inside the pump.*) It was a quite a tiring journey.

He kneels down to the bike.

CAROL. Are you from round this area then?

MARTIN. I live in Redcar, but was brought up in Middlesbrough. (*Trying to screw the connecting pipe to the front wheel.*) In his spare time my father was projectionist at the Grand Electric and eventually they gave us a house across the road. It's been knocked down now.

CAROL. That must be nice.

MARTIN *is fiddling with the wheel.*

A slight pause.

I'm a clerk in the tax office in Middlesbrough.

MARTIN. I know who to come to.

CAROL. Everybody sez that. Your tax will be handled somewhere else.

MARTIN. Something must be wrong with the thread.

He tries to screw the connecting pipe again.

Well I don't know.

CAROL. Have you tried blowing on it? Jack blows on everything.

MARTIN *blows into the thread of the connecting pipe. He tries again.*

MARTIN. No. I think I'll have to screw it on regardless.

CAROL. Try the back one first, it sometimes 'elps if you leave it.

MARTIN. That's a good idea – show it we're not defeated.

CAROL *stands up.* MARTIN *moves across to the back wheel.*

CAROL. What does your wife do?

MARTIN. She's a librarian.

He screws the connecting pipe to the back wheel without difficulty.

CAROL. Sounds like a sign of the zodiac when you say it like that.

MARTIN *smiles, he stands up, he has the pump in his hand.*

MARTIN. D'you believe in all that?

CAROL. I read my horoscope sometimes.

MARTIN (*screwing the pump to the connecting pipe*). My daughter-in-law goes to a palmist.

CAROL. I've never done that.

MARTIN. You're very wise. She pays him a fortune and he tells her she'll live a long and happy life. It's a lot to pay for reassurance.

CAROL. When a was younger I bought a book about tea leaves.

MARTIN *starts to pump up the tyre.*

MARTIN. The world of the tea bag has put a stop to all that.

CAROL *smiles.* MARTIN *stops pumping for a moment.*

I shouldn't make fun, should I?

CAROL. I don't care.

MARTIN *starts to pump again.*

MARTIN. I thought maybe you were very keen?

CAROL. No.

A slight pause.

MARTIN *feels the tyre.*

MARTIN. It's going up very slowly.

CAROL. Let us 'ave a go. Go on.

CAROL *starts to pump.* MARTIN *stands beside her.* CAROL *pumps faster than* MARTIN.

A pause.

MARTIN *watches her for a moment and then looks out to sea. He waves at someone on a boat.*

A slight pause.

MARTIN *waves again.*

MARTIN. He can't see me.

MARTIN *waves again.*

The shrill, loud 'bleep' of an oystercatcher.

MARTIN *puts his hands to his eyes and looks.*

There's an oystercatcher somewhere.

CAROL. That might do.

She stops pumping and feels the tyre.

I'll give it six more –

She starts to pump.

– five, six.

She feels the tyre.

Is that enough?

MARTIN *feels the tyre.*

MARTIN. That's perfect, thank you very much.

CAROL (*she looks hot*). I'll let you unscrew it.

MARTIN *takes the pump, he starts to unscrew it.*

MARTIN. What did your horoscope say for today?

CAROL. Which one? I saw the *Daily Express* at me mam's an' we take the *Mail*. Both said somethin' completely different. They're never bad though, a'they?

MARTIN (*standing up, the pump in his hand*). No.

The shrill, loud 'bleep' of an oystercatcher.

There it is again. It's somewhere.

He takes two Glacier Fruits from his jacket pocket.

Would you like one of these?

CAROL. Ta.

CAROL *takes one. They take off the wrappers.*

MARTIN. Give me your paper – (*Putting them in his pocket.*) I'll put them in my pocket.

He takes off his jacket.

(*Hanging his jacket on the nail.*) We had a lovely time in South Devon. It's a beautiful part of the country.

CAROL. Is it?

MARTIN. Everything is so much greener, I don't know why.

He bends down to the front tyre.

I wonder whether I ought to leave this and walk back.

CAROL. It's a long walk t'Redcar.

For a moment the faint sound of the demonstration.

MARTIN. Listen to them. At the steel plant. (*Standing up.*) I think there are more troublemakers than there are actual demonstrators.

Both are looking towards the steel plant.

Can you hear them?

CAROL. Yeah.

MARTIN. I didn't know what was happening until I walked past just now. Most of them are fifteen-year-olds looking for anything that might happen. They're shouting at each wagon as it goes in. I watched them for a while. Half of them I used to teach.

The sound of the crowd again.

A slight pause.

They've not got the willpower to think of anything better to do.

The crowd fades.

CAROL. I was wonderin' if Jack might've gone there.

MARTIN. I wasn't meaning the likes of him, I was meaning the youngsters. It's easy to criticise, I know.

CAROL. There's three of 'em really. They've been there all week.

The sound of the flute, as before.

MARTIN *changes position, he looks along the shore, his hands are in front of his eyes, shielding the light.*

MARTIN. There's a cormorant. On the shore.

CAROL *looks*.

CAROL. The bad weather's bringin' in all the birds.

A slight pause.

MARTIN. It's found a dead fish look.

A slight pause.

CAROL. So it 'as.

A slight pause.

MARTIN (*to himself as much as* CAROL). What will happen?
If they don't move the pipe?

A slight pause.

CAROL. Did it jus' swallow that whole?

MARTIN. Yes.

CAROL. That's the way to eat, isn't it.

MARTIN. They've a digestive system that's far better than ours.

CAROL. It needs t'be.

*The sound of the flute, slightly quicker and faster than
before.*

MARTIN (*pointing*). There it goes.

CAROL. It can still fly an' all.

They follow it. MARTIN *still has his hands in front of his
eyes. They follow it to the German Skerries.*

Silence.

MARTIN *waves his hands above his head.*

MARTIN. There's Michael. I think it's him in his boat.

CAROL *looks at him for a brief moment.* MARTIN *waves
again.*

Whoever it is, he's waving back.

He lowers his hand.

I'm sorry, my dear. Michael was at school with my eldest son. I see him occasionally.

CAROL *walks and picks up her book off the grass, she walks back.*

CAROL. 'Adn't you better get doin' your tyres?

MARTIN. I suppose I had.

CAROL (*bending down to the front wheel*). I'll do it.

MARTIN. I can manage.

CAROL (*putting the book on the grass beside her*). It's alright – it's sommat t'do while I'm waitin'.

She picks up the pump.

What else did yer dad do? Yer said 'e did that cinema work part time?

MARTIN. He was a bookseller with a little shop on Newport Road. Naturally when people couldn't afford food, they couldn't afford books. He made a little money from the wealthier folk but not enough to keep us all going. In the evening he took part-time work so as to be able to open his shop during the day.

CAROL *is fiddling with the pump and tyre.*

Books were his passion. That's what he wanted. We admired him for it.

CAROL. Yeah?

MARTIN. I don't think you're having much success?

CAROL. I'm not – it's 'opeless. We need John.

MARTIN (*bending down*). John?

CAROL (*still fiddling*). Jack – because 'e was small at school 'e used t'get bullied, 'e took to callin' himself Jack.

MARTIN. Leave it, my dear, I'll quite happily walk.

CAROL. I'm not beaten. (*Dropping the pump.*) It's 'opeless.

MARTIN. Let me have one last try.

> CAROL *moves out of the way.* MARTIN *tries.*

No.

> *He continues to fiddle.*

> CAROL *is still kneeling.*

CAROL. That's what a keep tellin' John 'e should do. He should do what he wants.

MARTIN. Pardon, my dear?

CAROL. Like your father.

MARTIN. It's the best way.

CAROL. That's what I tell 'im. 'E goes an' gets the cotton wool from the bathroom when a go on a lot and puts some in 'is ears.

MARTIN (*after a moment's pause*). The other side of the argument, you know, is that these things don't matter.

CAROL. What?

MARTIN. Nothing matters. Nothing is important.

CAROL. Why?

MARTIN. Because in the end it isn't. I'll let you into a secret, my dear, I realised something on holiday. It was that.

> *He is still fiddling.*

(*Smiling.*) I also realised something else – I'm getting old.

CAROL (*smiling*). Yer not.

MARTIN (*smiling. Fiddling*). Don't say I'm not when I say I am.

CAROL. How're you old?

MARTIN. I'm fifty-nine.

CAROL. That's not old. Me dad's nearly that.

MARTIN. How old's your dad?

CAROL. 'Bout fifty-four.

MARTIN. There's a lot of difference.

CAROL. Five years.

MARTIN (*smiling*). I can't argue with you, I can see.

CAROL. Yer can't when yer say that.

MARTIN (*still fiddling*). I've given up.

CAROL. Good.

MARTIN (*after a moment's pause*). Nothing is ever again going to get me down – that's old age.

CAROL *smiles*.

CAROL. I think that's great.

MARTIN (*pleased*). Do you?

CAROL. Yeah. It's wonderful.

MARTIN. I'm pleased. Life is too short. And I've lived most of mine.

He stands up.

I'm going to leave that as well and walk. It's been more trouble than it's worth.

CAROL *stands up*.

CAROL. What would yer do with John then? I've tried an' tried. You've met 'im? I can't ask my mam and dad, they don't understand. I know f' some o' the time 'e isn't 'appy.

MARTIN *puts the connecting pipe inside the pump*.

MARTIN. With what, my dear?

CAROL. I know it's not me, but –

A slight pause.

Sometimes I mekk mesel believe it is. That's something I can do somethin' about. Did 'e tell you 'e'd applied for a course? The letter came this mornin'. I 'aven't dared open it. I'll scream if it sez no.

MARTIN *puts the pump on his bike.*

He suffers a bit because of 'is school reports.

MARTIN *turns to her.*

MARTIN. Another thing I've learnt, my dear, is never to give advice. I think you'd be likely to take it and I don't want that. He's very nice your young man, hold on to him, so few people in this world are.

CAROL. Like me dad. John's right.

From the steel plant the sound of the crowd. MARTIN *and* CAROL *look toward it.*

MARTIN. I wonder what's going on down there? It sounds like trouble. The world isn't a rational place. Things aren't changed by rational people. (*After a moment's pause.*) I don't want to know.

A slight pause.

It'll be those local yobbos throwing stones. (*In despair.*) Oh dear. (*After a moment's pause.*) I feel a sadness.

Faintly, the sound of a police siren.

(*To himself.*) Why can't things be left alone.

CAROL. The police're there. I 'ope John isn't.

MARTIN (*to* CAROL). Why can't things be left alone?

CAROL. I don't know.

They watch.

The crowd can still be heard.

MARTIN. Perhaps if I could only see one side of an argument I might be down there myself.

CAROL. It's the yobbos who are breaking it up.

A slight pause.

MARTIN. Unfortunately I know the reason for that monstrosity. Teesside needs the jobs.

The sound of the crowd fades.

CAROL. They'll take 'em away.

The police siren stops. Silence.

MARTIN *undoes his saddlebag and takes out his cycle clips. He slowly and carefully puts them on.*

MARTIN (*realising*). What am I doing, I don't need these.

He takes them off and puts them back in the saddlebag. He looks towards the German Skerries.

(*Pointing.*) There's the cormorant on the German Skerries look.

CAROL (*looking*). Yes.

MARTIN *waves.*

MARTIN (*calling*). Michael. I don't think it is him. Never mind.

He smiles.

Give me a kiss, you're a very beautiful young lady.

CAROL *smiles.* MARTIN *kisses her on the cheek.*

(*Taking hold of his handlebars.*) The cormorant'll never nest there again.

He turns his bike round.

JACK *enters. He is carrying his shoes and socks in his left hand, his jeans are rolled up to his knees and his feet and ankles are covered in black oily mud. He is wearing a blue T-shirt. In his left hand he has his telescope and his* Hamlyn Bird Guide. *His binoculars are hanging round his neck.*

CAROL. D'you know what you look like?

JACK. Yeah, the bionic man.

He moves in slow motion.

CAROL (*to* MARTIN). Men think they rule this world. If it wasn't for women 'e'd stay like that all day long. D'you know what time it is?

JACK *looks at his watch.*

JACK. Five t'twelve, it's workin'.

MARTIN. Is it? I must be off – Ann is preparing my dinner – woe betide if I'm late.

He wheels the bike forward.

JACK. Are you comin' back this af'ernoon?

MARTIN. I might be.

JACK. I'll see yer then then.

CAROL. No, you won't.

MARTIN *has stopped.*

JACK. 'As she told yer where we're goyn?

MARTIN. No.

JACK (*to* CAROL). We're goyn t'South Devon, aren't we?

CAROL (*smiling. To* MARTIN). Yes.

MARTIN. On holiday?

JACK. Yes.

CAROL. We won't make it if you don't get a move-on.

MARTIN (*wheeling his bike forward*). Enjoy yourselves.

JACK. Tarra.

CAROL. Tarra.

MARTIN *exits.*

JACK (*calling after him*). See you this afternoon.

CAROL. No you won't, John.

JACK. Yes, I will.

CAROL. Where've yer bin?

JACK. There was a flock of dunlin on the mudflats.

CAROL. I didn't think yerd bin to Timbuktu – I've been 'ere ages. 'Ave yer been down there?

JACK. Where?

CAROL. You know, the steel plant.

JACK. I wen' an' 'ad a look.

CAROL. I bet yer did.

JACK. I wanted to 'ave a look. That's the good news, isn't it – they're gonna move the pipe.

CAROL *smiles*.

Me birdwatchin's safe f'ever.

He puts all his things on the grass.

CAROL. That's good.

JACK (*smiling*). It is, isn't it. The cormorants'll be able to nest. They're shovin' the pipe on two 'undred yards.

CAROL (*smiling*). That's really good.

JACK. Course it is.

CAROL. What was all the noise about then?

JACK. When I left the committee were gonna call the police cos of all them lads throwin' rocks.

CAROL. Not you I hope?

JACK. No, not me. The meetin' was goin' on inside. Just as I was leavin' they sent out a note, they'd won. Fantastic.

CAROL. All that trouble.

JACK. The cormorants will be able to nest. The pipe'll be too far on to stop them. The fishermen are happy 'n' all. Everybody's 'appy.

CAROL. I've bin t'see me mam, we're 'avin tea there before we set off.

JACK *looks at her.*

Don't pull a face at me.

JACK. Seein' as it's the holiday.

CAROL. What else could I say when she asked?

JACK. I suppose so.

CAROL. We've got to get packed up.

JACK. I want to come back 'ere – there's dunlin.

CAROL. I want to leave the house straight before we go as well
   – I don't want to come back to a mess. If a don't get it
   straight, that's all I'll think about.

JACK sits down.

Look at you.

JACK. Can yer get me a towel – a put one in the car.

CAROL. Am I your slave?

JACK. Yes.

*Faintly from the distance, the bugle-like call of a herring
gull.*

CAROL. I'm not, you know.

She starts to exit, she stops.

I've 'ad it on my mind all this time an' now I've forgotten.

She walks to the hut and picks up the book.

There's a letter fo' yer.

JACK (*slightly worried*). What? From work?

*CAROL takes an envelope from inside the book, it has an
ICI insignia embossed on it. She stands beside him.*

CAROL (*giving him the letter*). It came in the second post. I
   'ope it sez what you want it to.

JACK holds the letter.

Go on, open it.

JACK. I don't want to. It might be bad.

CAROL. It's your letter.

A slight pause.

JACK. 'Ere goes.

He tears open the envelope. Slowly he takes out the letter.

CAROL. Read it then.

JACK *opens out the letter, he reads. His face drops.*

JACK (*quietly*). 'E's a bastard that man. Why couldn' 'e tell me to me face? I saw 'im on Fridi.

CAROL *takes the letter from his hand, she starts to read it.*

(*Upset.*) Why couldn' 'e, Carol?

A slight pause.

That about finishes me off wi' the bloody job, I'm tellin' yer. I was bankin' on that. All the plans and everything. Let me see it agen.

CAROL *gives* JACK *the letter.*

CAROL. I'm sorry, love.

JACK *looks at the letter.*

JACK. My aptitude to work – what does that mean?

CAROL (*looking over his shoulder*). Is it aptitude or attitude?

JACK. Aptitude – I work bloody 'ard, Carol.

CAROL *is re-reading the letter over his shoulder.*

I wouldn've minded if 'e could 'ave told me to me bloody face.

CAROL. He says your aptitude to work is good.

JACK. It's like a fuckin' school report. I do know all about it, Carol, I do.

CAROL *finishes reading the letter.*

CAROL. Apart from the fact that he's not going to send you on the course it's quite a nice letter.

JACK. Nice, my arse.

CAROL (*angry*). Oh, shut up, John! And stop usin' words like that. Why don't yer listen to what he's got t'say at the end. What does he say about O levels?

JACK *is stunned into silence.*

Why don't yer?

JACK. I can't.

CAROL. How d'you know if you've never tried?

JACK. A don't 'ave t'run into a fire t'know I'd burn, do I?

CAROL. That's not the same thing, and you know it.

JACK. Do I? I don't.

CAROL. Stop being childish.

JACK. It's alright f' you, isn't it? Fine 'igh an' miss mighty. Wi' everythin' that I 'aven't got.

He screws the letter into a ball.

Mekks yer sick.

He gets up and walks away.

Yer can keep yer mouth shut an' all.

CAROL *looks at him.* JACK *has his back to her.*

Silence.

CAROL. Why not do one? Just to start with?

JACK. I could do twenty million.

A slight pause.

Which one would a do?

CAROL. Do chemistry. Something you're interested in.

JACK. Physics. It'd take me hours.

CAROL. Jus' think 'ow you'd feel when you'd done it.

JACK. Knackered.

A slight pause.

I want t'do one more than you.

A slight pause.

(*Repentant.*) No, a don't.

He turns to face her.

I probably could do physics, I know about physics. A wouldn't pass though.

CAROL. Yer would if yer put yer mind to it, John, and concentrated.

JACK. It's jus' we goin' on 'oliday – it would 'ave to come today.

CAROL. Never mind that.

JACK. All them brainy kids doin' 'em – it'd be like goyn back to school.

CAROL. That doesn't matter.

JACK. Well.

CAROL. Well what?

JACK. Well it would. Brainy idiots.

CAROL. You know you're as good as any of them.

JACK. Do I?

CAROL. Of course you are.

JACK. I'm not yer see, Carol, that's the trouble.

CAROL. You are. You've got to learn to believe in yourself.

JACK. 'Ow can I do that, if I can't?

CAROL. Well you 'ave a good try f' a start-off.

JACK. What 'appens if I can't then?

CAROL. You're making problems.

JACK. I'm not.

CAROL. You are, John.

JACK *opens out the crumpled letter, he looks at it.*

JACK. It's a shit. D'yer think I could pass three? 'E says three.

CAROL. Yes.

A slight pause.

And if you can't, John, at least you'd know.

A slight pause.

JACK. I wanted promotion, Carol. I really did. More then everything else. I'd 'ave even given up me birdwatching – they could 'ave built that pipe for all I cared.

CAROL. You'll get it, don't worry.

JACK. I might do. Perhaps.

CAROL. There's no perhaps about it. Half the battle with these things is confidence. Believe you will, and you will.

JACK. D'yer reckon?

CAROL. Yes.

A slight pause.

Just think how you'll feel.

A slight pause.

JACK (*smiling*). Yer wanna mekk me into a snob.

CAROL. I'll let you use that word just once more.

JACK. Come 'ere, snob.

CAROL *walks to him.*

I'll rip the page with snob on from the dictionary.

CAROL. That's twice.

JACK. I'll do two, eh? Chemistry and physics, jus' to prove it.

Very, very faintly, the sound of the sea can be heard rolling against the shore.

Fetch us the towel. It's on the back seat.

CAROL. I hope you're going to thank my dad.

JACK. I 'ave done.

CAROL. I am sorry. (*Hugs him.*)

JACK. Enough said, eh? I saw that old man kissin' yer.

CAROL. I'll get you a towel.

CAROL *exits.*

A slight pause.

JACK *looks through his binoculars and turns round in a full circle. He takes them from round his neck, sits down, puts them on the grass and puts the letter back in the envelope. The shrill, loud 'bleep' of an oystercatcher.*

JACK. An oystercatcher.

He raises his telescope and looks through it.

A slight pause.

CAROL *enters, carrying a white towel and wearing an old German war helmet. She creeps up behind JACK, walks past him and puts her face in front of the telescope. JACK jumps out of his skin, he does a backward somersault and ends in a standing position. CAROL smiles.*

Bloody 'ell – Carol.

CAROL. I found it while I was waitin' .

JACK. Phew.

CAROL *laughs.*

Phew. I'll think of somethin' t'do t'you one day – just you wait.

CAROL. 'Ere's the towel.

JACK *takes the towel.*

JACK. Right.

He puts the towel over his head and acts like a ghost. He wanders about, moaning.

I am the ghost that haunts you. I am the phantom birdwatcher.

*He is near the hut, he pretends to pick something up. He
throws the towel off.*

Right. What 'ave I got in 'ere?

CAROL (*backing away*). John.

JACK. I'm going to put it in your hair.

CAROL (*backing away*). John.

JACK (*getting near her*). I'm going to make you eat it – spider
and chips.

CAROL. John.

JACK *opens his palm, he pretends to throw, his palm is
empty.*

(*Running away.*) John.

JACK *sits down and starts to clean his feet with the towel.*

You're rotten.

CAROL *still has the helmet on, she sits down beside him.*

JACK (*smiling*). I know.

CAROL (*after a moment's pause*). I was rotten first, I'll forgive
you.

JACK. I want t'buy yer dad a bottle of whisky f' lettin' us take
'is car. We'll get that, then I'll pick the tent up.

CAROL. Right. I'm not tekkin' food, I've decided, we'll buy it
there.

JACK. It's a bloody long way t'drive.

CAROL. An' we've gotta be at me mam's f' five.

JACK. We can give yer dad 'is whisky then.

CAROL *notices* MARTIN'*s jacket which is still hanging on
the nail.*

CAROL. He's left 'is jacket?

JACK *is still vigorously cleaning his feet.*

JACK. Has he? 'E must 'ave a memory like a sieve.

CAROL *absent-mindedly looks through the pockets.*

CAROL. What d'yer think we should do?

JACK. Put it in the hut – 'e'll find it.

CAROL *does so, she comes out and stands beside* JACK.

CAROL. 'E didn't know you know, John.

JACK. What about?

CAROL. About his friend – well, his son's friend. I didn't tell him either.

JACK *starts to put on his socks.* CAROL *sits down beside him.*

Your feet are in a hell of a state.

JACK. lt doesn't matter.

A slight pause.

CAROL. 'E told me we were a nice couple. I've a feelin' 'e lives f' this place.

She stands, walks, picks up her book and comes back.

JACK. l'm rushin' as it is.

The shrill, loud 'bleep' of an oystercatcher.

JACK *starts to put on his shoes.*

I 'ope Salcombe's as good as he sez it is.

The bugle-like call of a herring gull.

JACK *is fastening his laces.*

The sound of the flute, as before.

The lights quickly fade.

The End.

A Nick Hern Book

This edition of *German Skerries* first published in Great Britain in 2016 by Nick Hern Books Limited, The Glasshouse, 49a Goldhawk Road, London W12 8QP, in association with the Orange Tree Theatre, Richmond, and Up in Arms

German Skerries first published in Great Britain in 1977 by Heinemann Educational Books Ltd, in the volume *German Skerries & Mud*

Cover photo: Shutterstock; design: Annie Rushton

Designed and typeset by Nick Hern Books, London
Printed in Great Britain by Mimeo Ltd, Cambridgeshire PE29 6XX

A CIP catalogue record for this book is available from the British Library

ISBN   978 1 84842 547 7